THE REMARKABLE LIFE OF
BISHOP BONAVENTURE BRODERICK

THE REMARKABLE LIFE
of
BISHOP BONAVENTURE BRODERICK

Exile,
Redemption,
and a Gas Station

James K. Hanna

PITTSBURGH:
Serif Press
2022

© James K. Hanna 2022

Serif Press
serifpress.com

For Alice, editor extraordinaire

Preface and Acknowledgements

Call it "search engine providence." I read in Gerald Nicosia's biography of Jack Kerouac (*Memory Babe*, University of California Press, 1983) that Thomas Merton and Kerouac were together at a party hosted by New York photographer Robert Frank, circa 1960. Really...? I went online to search out Nicosia's contact information to ask him his source. I also began searching for other references to any meeting of the two Catholic writers.

I don't recall the combinations of words and names I used in multiple searches but one included St. Bonaventure University where Merton once taught. I kept pulling the thread and as the internet unraveled, a story popped up about a character named Bonaventure Broderick, a Roman Catholic bishop; not just a bishop, but a bishop who ran a gas station for many years in the small town of Millbrook, New York. Really...? This was more intriguing to me than the alleged Merton-Kerouac meeting. And so began an adventure that took me on the road to the Hudson Valley and Millbrook, Washington Hollow, Hawthorne, and Yonkers; to people, places, and things—to archivists, priests, historical societies, and cemeteries; to vacant lots and antique shops and yes, to a gas station. I soon found that this was a story worthy of my obsession; that Bonaventure Broderick's life was a life worth knowing.

I met many gracious people on the road, online, by telephone, and through the mail, who gave freely of their time and knowledge; this project could not have been completed without them.

Thanks to all the kind folks in Millbrook: Father Hartley Bancroft, pastor of St. Joseph Church; Robert McHugh and Alison Meyer of the Millbrook Historical Society; Kevin DeMartine, who owns an antique shop on Washington Hollow Road and whose mother purchased Broderick's gas station from Helen Bowlen; and the Millbrook Library staff for their help finding Broderick's *Millbrook Round Table* columns.

I am grateful to Paul Dvorchak for his critical eye; to Mike Aquilina, Christopher Bailey, Ron Hansen, and Rob Mitrik for their advice, support, and encouragement along the way; to Kate Feighery, archivist at the Archdiocese of New York, for her hospitality and for kindly contacting me when the archives reopened following the COVID shutdown; to Father Michael Morris, former archivist of the archdiocese, a genial host who spent the better part of a morning with me in Hyde Park at Regina Coeli Church; and to Joshua Mark for helping me find the Broderick home in nearby Staatsburg.

Thanks to Monsignor Thomas M. Ginty for sending me a copy of his 1989 master's thesis; to J. Ogden Tyldsley, Jr., for his correspondence and memories of his parents' friendship with Bishop Broderick; and to Terry Phelan, Bonaventure's first cousin three times removed, whose extensive research into her family tree and our frequent correspondence was so helpful.

To the many archivists and others who were patient with my multiple requests: Monte Abbot at the Sisters of the Good Shepherd in St. Louis; Alison Foley at Associated Archives at St. Mary's Seminary and University; Chet Kerr, at the Irvington,

NY Historical Society; Rena Schergan, archivist, Archdiocese of St. Louis; Patrick Shank, archivist, Archdiocese of Philadelphia; Stephanie Shreffler at the University of Dayton's Roesch Library; Paul Spaeth at St. Bonaventure University's Friedsam Library; Michelle Tom, librarian and archivist at the Windsor, CT Historical Society; Sarah Waits at the Archdiocese of New Orleans archives; Kathleen Washy, archivist, Sisters of St. Joseph, Baden, PA; Dennis Wodzinski, archivist at the Diocese of Pittsburgh; and Bridgette A. Woodall, archivist, Archdiocese of Hartford. They helped make the task of research and writing an enjoyable venture and I thank them all.

Contents

Major Characters xiv

Introduction xxii

1. Early Life and Education, 1868–1898 1

2. Fast Start and First Troubles in Connecticut, 1898–1900 .. 11

3. The War with Spain 19

4. Cuba and the Road to the Episcopacy, 1900–1903 29

5. Rumors and the Grave Misunderstanding, 1904–1905 43

6. Early Years of Exile, 1905–1911 59

7. More Turmoil: Gossip and Legal Drama, 1912–1915 77

8. Quiet Times, 1915–1926 101

9. A Phantom Hot Dog Stand and the Fabled Gas Station, 1926–1939 111

10. End of Exile, 1939 123

11. Reconciled Years, 1940-1943 141

Bibliography 159

Notes 161

Major Characters

Bonaventure Finnbarr Broderick (1868–1943)

Three Named Margaret

Many well-known persons, including politicians and popes, surface in the life of Bonaventure Broderick, but three lesser-known women, all christened Margaret, play significant roles. We meet them on the pages that follow, and an introductory glance will be helpful, in the order of their appearance in his life.

Margaret (Healy) Broderick (1835–1917) Bonaventure's mother, Margaret Healy, was born in Ireland in 1830. She married John Harris Broderick, also Irish-born, who came to America in 1850, at age fifteen. She was widowed at age seventy in 1900, after her youngest son was ordained a priest and before he became a bishop. Beginning in 1900, Bonaventure took his mother under his care until her death at age eighty-seven in 1917, in Saugerties, New York, where the bishop purchased a large estate, naming it *Villa Marguerite* in her honor.

Margaret Josephine (Loughman) Graves, formerly Plant (1844–1909) Born in 1844, Margaret Loughman married the widowed Henry B. Plant, a millionaire industrialist, in 1874. In the late 1890's she met Father Broderick in Branford, Connecticut, providing him with a significant monetary contribution towards the construction of a new church. Henry Plant died in 1899 and Margaret subsequently married another millionaire, Robert Graves. When Margaret died in 1909, she named Bishop Broderick one of many beneficiaries of her estate and a co-executor.

Margaret Helen Bowlen (ca. 1880–1949) A bit of mystery veils our third Margaret. For starters, she will be known throughout as "Helen." In 1897, nineteen-year-old Margaret Helen Bowlen entered a St. Louis, Missouri convent as a novice in the Congregation of the Sisters of Charity of the Good Shepherd, taking the religious name Sister Mary of St. Helena. Two years later she professed her temporary vows, renewable annually and was sent to Cuba to assist in the operation of a newly opened reform school for girls. In 1901 she "returned to the world"[1] to care for Margaret Broderick. Her presence in the Broderick household led to rumor; the scandalous gossip became part of the story of the impeachment of the governor of New York in 1912 and led to an investigation by the Church into the bishop's marital status. After Margaret Broderick died, Helen remained in the home as housekeeper. Over the years she owned multiple parcels of real estate, including that of the fabled gas station.

Siblings

Clement Broderick (1865–1903) The older of Bonaventure's two brothers, Clement was an inventor who founded an ammunition factory in Windsor, Connecticut. Complications surrounding the circumstances of the eventual failure of the business significantly affected the trajectory of Bonaventure's priesthood. Clement died before his brother became a bishop.

David Broderick (1866–1940) An engineer by training, he partnered with Clement in operating and financing the ammunition factory until its failure. He then became a manufacturer's representative for Unionville businesses before going to work for Bonaventure and John A. Sullivan (Donovan & Phillips Co.) as the manager of a construction project in Cuba. The financially rich construction contract would lead to division and litigation between the brothers.

Mentors

Orazio Marucchi (1852–1931) Italian archaeologist and author of the *Manual of Christian Archaeology*, he was a mentor to Broderick during his seminary days in Rome and together they participated in significant archaeological discoveries.

Henry Ruthven Monteith (1848–1922) Monteith was a high school teacher of Broderick and later served as professor of history and English at Connecticut Agricultural College (now the University of Connecticut). The two kept a friendship until Monteith's death.

Denis J. O'Connell (1849–1927) O'Connell, a confidante, was Rector of the North American College in Rome when

Broderick was in attendance. He was later named Bishop of Richmond, Virginia.

Among the Church Hierarchy

Placide Chapelle (1842–1905) Chapelle, the French-born Archbishop of New Orleans, Louisiana, was appointed Apostolic Delegate to Cuba and the Philippines following the Spanish-American War. He leveled the charges against Broderick that led to his long exile.

Amleto Cicognani (1883–1973) Archbishop Cicognani, as Apostolic Delegate, played a vital role in triggering the extraordinary events that led to Bishop Broderick's reconciliation with the Church.

John Farley (1842–1918) In 1912, as Archbishop of New York, Cardinal Farley launched an investigation into rumors that Bishop Broderick was married.

James Gibbons (1834–1921) Cardinal Gibbons of Baltimore was the leading American prelate at the crucial moment when Broderick faced charges of impropriety. Gibbons' negative opinion of Broderick influenced the Vatican's treatment of the young bishop.

Leo XIII (1810–1903) Pope from 1878—1903, he honored Father Broderick with the title monsignor in 1901 in recognition of his accomplishment in the settlement of church property in Cuba.

Raphael Merry del Val (1865–1930) Merry del Val received the cardinal's hat from Pius X in November of 1903 and was named Secretary of State. The following month he influenced the exile of Bishop Broderick, who felt the Cardinal was hostile to him.

Pius X (1835–1914) Successor to Leo XIII, Pius X was central to the misunderstanding that exiled Broderick in 1905. For reasons unknown, it appears the Holy Father never communicated with Bishop Broderick after 1905.

Michael Tierney (1839–1908) Tierney was the Bishop of Hartford when Broderick was ordained in Rome. Less than two years after Father Broderick returned from Rome Tierney made an investment in Clement Broderick's business. The business was eventually bankrupted, and the fallout ruptured the bishop-priest relationship.

Donato Sbarretti (1856–1939) The Italian-born Sbarretti was a professor in Rome when he first encountered Broderick as a young seminarian-student. Later, when Sbarretti became Bishop of Havana, he took Father Broderick with him as his American Secretary. Sbarretti continued to rise in the Church, eventually elevated to Cardinal and Secretary of the Congregation of the Holy Office. Sbarretti triggered the events that led to Spellman's great act of charity in bringing Broderick back to the Church.

Francis Spellman (1889–1967) In a true act of charity, one of the first tasks Spellman undertook in 1939 as the newly consecrated Archbishop of New York was to seek out Bishop Broderick, in near-secrecy, to reconcile him with the Church.

Politicians and Men of Industry

Pablo Desvernine (ca. 1852–1935) A lawyer, professor, and diplomat, Desvernine served as Minister of Finance for Cuba during the United States occupation following the Spanish-American War. He and Broderick remained lifelong friends.

Simon Donovan (1854–1911) and George Phillips (1855—1912) The two Boston businessmen owned the Donovan & Phillips Co., a construction company that was purchased in 1908 by Bishop Broderick and John A. Sullivan.

Mark A. Hanna (1837–1904) A millionaire by age forty, the U.S. Senator from Ohio was a political favorite of Broderick's whose influence he sought in negotiations with Washington about the settlement of Church property.

Hugh J. Reilly, Sr. (1844–1920) Reilly was a New York contractor and held the general contract for the construction of the Cienfuegos aqueduct project for which the Donovan & Phillips Co. was a subcontractor.

Elihu Root (1845–1937) Root served as Secretary of War under both President McKinley and Theodore Roosevelt. He and Broderick formed a friendship during Broderick's early years in Cuba.

Theodore Roosevelt (1858–1919) The twenty-sixth president of the United States, Roosevelt was instrumental in helping Broderick establish the Italian American Agriculture Association in 1905.

John A. Sullivan (1868–1927) Sullivan was member of the U.S House of Representatives (11th District, Massachusetts) from 1903 -1907. In 1908 he and Bishop Broderick assumed joint ownership of the Donovan & Phillips Co.

Major Characters

William Sulzer (1863–1941) "Plain Bill" was chosen Governor of New York in 1913 and impeached in 1914. Bishop Broderick played a pivotal role in Sulzer's fall from grace.

Amasa Pierce Thornton (1854–1917) Thornton was a New York lawyer well connected with the Vatican. He undertook an investigation in 1905 of Broderick's "Peter's Pence" appointment, reporting his findings to Gibbons.

John O. Tyldsley (1906–1960) Tyldsley was the publisher of the *Millbrook Round Table,* Millbrook, New York, the weekly newspaper that published Bishop Broderick's columns in the 1930's.

Leonard Wood (1860–1927) As Military Governor of Cuba, General Wood worked closely with Broderick, before and after he became a bishop, to settle questions of Church property in Cuba.

Introduction

A Connecticut native, Bonaventure F. Broderick spent several years running a gas station—as a bishop—his presence "a cause of wonderment for Catholics and non-Catholics alike."[2]

As a twenty-year-old, Broderick saw himself as a rising industrialist, his talents absorbed by business; one year later he entered the seminary, aiming instead at a life of caring for souls. At twenty-nine the young priest was an internationally recognized archaeologist. At thirty-two a pope named him a monsignor, and at thirty-four another made him a bishop. He was hailed as one of the brightest and most forceful men in the Church.[3]

Two years later he was persona non grata in Rome. At home, the leading American prelate, Cardinal James Gibbons, considered him a person from whom one should keep a distance.

And the Church did keep its distance, for thirty-four years, until 1939 when an extraordinary thing happened. Broderick, then seventy-years-old, was at home in his farmhouse behind his gas station when a surprise visitor knocked on the front door. When he opened it, he came face-to-face with fifty-year-old Francis Spellman, the newly consecrated Archbishop of New York.

The ensuing conversation was the beginning of the end of the long exile, leading to a reconciliation with the Church and a friendship so dear that Spellman proclaimed in 1942,

"The greatest thing I have done for my soul and the greatest gift I have brought to the people of the archdiocese has been in bringing Bishop Broderick to New York."[4]

At best, Bishop Broderick's life has been a curious footnote in the recorded history of the Church in America. As one archivist wrote the present author, "he appears to have lived a rather interesting life but remains a relatively mysterious man."[5]

Mysterious, yes, but also *undiscovered.*

For the few who know of him, it is the gas station they usually reference. It is an oddity that naturally attracts attention, but there is so much more to the story of this cleric who fell from grace at an early age, a victim of rumor and misunderstanding.

In these pages we confront head-on the central and complex character in what Francis Spellman's biographer, Robert Gannon, called "the strange and deeply moving case of the Most Reverend Bonaventure F. Broderick."[6]

In 1905, Broderick, his reputation tainted by gossip and accusations, was set adrift as a bishop without an assignment.

The story of his banishment is peculiar; his many years in exile fascinating; the tale of his reconciliation borders the miraculous, and the aftermath is heartening.

A respected and published archaeologist, a gifted wordsmith and orator, a practiced gardener and amateur horticulturist, a patron of the arts, a statesman and master of secular political connections, a seasoned fundraiser, and a man who loved and cared for his widowed, aging mother, Broderick never publicly spoke ill of the Church during his long exile. He also remained busy, earning enormous sums of money, and losing much of it until Spellman found him "eking out his existence by conducting a little business."[7]

There are no in-depth biographies, and a handful of books published late in the last century present few details of his life. Recent years have seen a nominal surge of interest fueled by short newspaper articles and internet blog postings with titles and content emphasizing, and often exaggerating, his time running a gas station.

During the early years the Ford Model T was coming off the assembly line Broderick was not pumping gas—or even using it: he was driving a 1910 steam-powered Stanley[8] and spending much of his time in courtrooms wrangling over legal and financial matters, either defending himself or trying to win six-figure lawsuits, one of which he brought against his own brother, another against a magazine for defamation.

The courtroom drama takes place ten years after his brief time (1903-1905) as Auxiliary Bishop of San Cristóbal de la Habana, Cuba, the episcopal appointment from which he was forced out, setting in motion his thirty-four-years-long exile.

The story has been told only in miniature; a sampling follows.

James Hennesey, in *American Catholics: A History of the Roman Catholic Community in the United States*,[9] published in 1981, mentions Broderick once, in reference to his time in Cuba: "Freed from Spain, the island became a political protectorate and vassal of the United States. American priests were sent to aid the local church, and Bonaventure Broderick, a Hartford priest, served briefly as auxiliary bishop of Havana."[10]

In *Patterns of Episcopal Leadership*,[11] published in 1989 we find Broderick mentioned in the essay "James Gibbons of Baltimore" where noted historian John Tracy Ellis outlines how Cardinal Gibbons disfavored Broderick who was among those Gibbons found "reason for distancing himself from."[12]

In Robert Gannon's 1962 *The Cardinal Spellman Story*[13] we find vital correspondence and greater detail of Spellman's rehabilitation effort.

Benedict Groeschel, in *Arise from Darkness*,[14] a 1995 collection of inspirational profiles, condenses Broderick's life to three pages. Alas, the bishop's name is misspelled throughout, and the claim made that he invented and patented "a funny little gadget on the end of the pump nozzle that caused it to stop automatically when the tank was full."[15]

The most extensive treatment, including interviews with several people who knew Bishop Broderick, is found in a forty-page master's thesis written in 1989 by a seminarian of Mount St. Mary's at Emmittsburg, Maryland. That seminarian is today a priest of the Archdiocese of Hartford, Connecticut, Monsignor Thomas M. Ginty.[16]

I read and profited from them all, and a few others, but was left with a nagging curiosity about what had been omitted, left unexplored or was simply inaccurate; a hunch that there was more to learn and details to correct. My instincts were right.

The gas station is little more than a sidebar. His is a story of catacombs in Rome, a failed bomb-building business in Connecticut and a sewer system in Cuba.

It is a story of allegations, from the serious to the sensational to the silly: that he shared in a million-dollar commission to sell Church property in Havana; that he was living with "a nun he stole from a convent in St. Louis;" that he was "running a hot dog stand" in upstate New York.

It is a story of a millionaire Congregationalist and his Catholic wife, an impeached governor of New York, quarreling siblings and quibbling Church hierarchy.

It is a tale of popes and politicians, business partners who throw inkwells at each other, and a lawyer who probes into a private papal conversation on behalf of a cardinal of the Church.

It is a chronicle of conflicts, complicated by politics, principles, and personalities.

In the following chapters readers will find a deeper dig into the life of a cleric who, dogged by uninvited controversies and rejected by the hierarchy, never loses heart, perseveres through decades of drama, and is eventually rewarded, spending the last few years of his life alongside Francis Spellman.

As with the story of any life some of what is true is left in oblivion, but in our quest for verifiable truth much of the mystery is resolved thanks to archived correspondence, sacramental records, census data, passenger manifests, affidavits, and the recorded understanding of events by long-deceased journalists at news services and papers such as the *Hartford Courant, New York Times, Washington Post,* and *Boston Globe.*

In these pages we encounter Broderick in all his complexity, "a finely educated man, of commanding appearance, standing six feet tall and weighing about 250 pounds," from boyhood to young industrialist in New England; to ordination in Rome; to his consecration as bishop, "the youngest American to wear the mitre;"[17] to his abrupt resignation in 1905 and severed ties with the Church; through years of courtroom drama to quieter times and his fabled gas station; to the knock on his door in 1939 and, finally, his return to the Church—the Church he never left—but the Church that left him.

1. Early Life and Education, 1868–1898

The Family in Connecticut

Bonaventure Finnbar Broderick was born on Christmas Day, 1868 in Hartford, Connecticut, the son of thirty-three-year-old John Harris Broderick, and thirty-eight-year-old Margaret (Healy) Broderick, both first generation Irish Americans.

He was one of nine children born of the marriage: six sons and three daughters. Six of the children died in infancy or childhood. Only Bonaventure and two older brothers, Clement, born in 1865, and David, in 1866, survived to adulthood.

The family lived in the second ward of Hartford, then an emergent city of 37,000. The city's first significant influx of immigrants was the Irish, who, like John Broderick, arrived in large numbers in the 1850's and worked mostly as unskilled laborers. In 1870 the total number of foreign born in Hartford was 10,343, including 7,438 Irish.[18]

John Broderick began his American experience as a farm laborer,[19] but over time he became "a wealthy and distinguished entrepreneur,"[20] setting an example of ambition and industry that each of his sons emulated in their own way. For Bonaventure, these character traits became a pattern for life, the fabric of his story.

When Bonaventure was twelve the family lived thirty miles southwest of Hartford, in Waterbury, a town of 15,000, where his parents owned and operated a boarding house on Harrisville Road,[21] where many of the lodgers were Irish men working on the railroad.[22]

By the mid-1880's, John Broderick's ambition was paying dividends and the family moved to Farmington, a town in the village of Unionville, fifteen miles west of Hartford, to a federal-style mansion previously owned by the late Lambert Hitchcock,[23] the innovative furniture manufacturer who became famous for the mass produced "Hitchcock chair."

In the U. S. Census of 1900[24] John Broderick's occupation is listed as "Manufacturer," his wealth acquired through investments in the local paper mill industry.[25] Unionville was a large smokestack community, home to four paper mills benefiting from the web of canals connected to the Farmington River and more than a dozen other companies producing a wide variety of products including machinery, hardware, tools, furniture, wood turnings, clocks, soap, candles, and musical instruments.[26] David Broderick, in time, would become a manufacturer's representative for many of these businesses.

Bonaventure's character was taking shape when he began working in the Unionville paper mills at age fourteen [27] while attending high school. He was gaining a reputation as a stellar student, learning the skills that would equip him for his future vocations while earning the admiration and respect of his instructors. First among these was Henry Ruthven Monteith, later a history professor and first to be given the title "professor emeritus" at what is now the University of Connecticut, where it was said "It had become an almost unwritten law that no man's education was finished until he had taken a course under Professor Monteith."²⁸ The student and his teacher, who will meet again in Chapter Eight, maintained a lifelong friendship.

By the time he graduated in 1886 he had five years' experience in papermaking. After high school he remained in Unionville for three years, working at paper mills ²⁹ there and in Holyoke, Massachusetts,³⁰ discerning his future while his older brothers were establishing themselves. David became an engineer and went off to Germany to manage a machine shop while Clement was an idea-man who had a knack for inventing things and worked as a foreman at Dwight Slate Machine Company.³¹

During this period Bonaventure, in his words, "achieved phenomenal success in the industrial world." But change was afoot. Perhaps it was the influence of his mother, a devout Catholic who attended Mass daily, the influence of a priest or religious sister, or simply the work of the Holy Spirit, but in 1889 he discerned a call to the priesthood and "voluntarily abandoned an assured future of wealth and distinction high-up in the papermaking industry, because, as a priest" he wished to devote his life "to the care of souls and the administration of the Sacraments."³²

Celebrated Scholar in Maryland and Rome

In September of 1889 he began his studies for the priesthood at St. Charles College at Ellicott City, Maryland. "Boni," as he was called by classmates, continued to excel in academics. His first year he received first prize in medieval history and honorable mention in English, poetry, and geometry, as well as first prize in Christian Doctrine and modern history, second prize in physiology, honorable mention in rhetoric, church history, solid geometry, and plane trigonometry; an impressive academic performance considering he entered a class that had been together four years.[33] He graduated *magna cum laude* in 1891.[34]

After graduation, and following a competitive examination,[35] Bishop Lawrence McMahon, the fifth bishop of Hartford, sent him to the North American College in Rome.[36] During this time, the young and affable seminarian established many enduring friendships, including that of Father Denis J. O'Connell, Rector of the college, and Monsignor Donato Sbaretti, his ethics professor. Both men will figure prominently in Broderick's future; O'Connell as an early confidante,[37] and Sbarretti as a mentor.

His time in the Eternal City occasioned another academic growth spurt as he continued to earn honors and the respect of faculty, including that of Sbarretti and Christianity's premier archaeologist, Dr. Orazio Marucchi who sparked his intense and rewarding interest in archaeology. He was also acquainted with and influenced by renowned archaeologists Giovanni Batista de Rossi and Mariano Armellini, one of the founders of the Pontifical Academy of Martyrs; the German scholar Theodor Mommsen; and historian Louis Duchesne,[38] who, like Broderick, was at the time an amateur archaeologist.

In 1893 he received a doctorate in philosophy and on July 26, 1896, was ordained to the priesthood by Archbishop Francesco di Paola Cassetta. Catalogues of the Propaganda from 1892–1896 show Broderick had the best record of American students of the period.[39]

After his ordination he remained in Rome to continue his studies in theology and archaeology before returning to Connecticut for the summer of 1897. When he arrived in Connecticut for the summer, he was greeted by sixty-year-old Bishop Michael Tierney,[40] the sixth bishop of Hartford, who assigned the young priest to the Cathedral of St. Joseph in Hartford[41] where he soon proved himself a gifted public speaker delivering many popular lectures at the Cathedral lyceum on a wide range of topics from archaeology to one titled "What the Church has Done for Women."[42]

He returned to Rome in the fall of 1897 to complete the degree of Doctor of Sacred Theology under the direction of Sbarretti. He then dedicated his time fully to continued studies in archaeology[43] under the direction of Dr. Marucchi, author of at least 500 works including the premier textbook *Manual of Christian Archaeology*. Marucchi served as Professor of Christian Archaeology at the University of Rome and director of the Christian and Egyptian museums at the Vatican Museums; was a member of the Pontifical Commission of Sacred Archaeology and a *scrittore* of the Vatican Library.

During his studies with Marucchi, Broderick was present for several discoveries in the Forum, the Roman plaza surrounded by ruins, and in the Roman catacombs, which attracted international attention. The *Catholic Times of London* reported on Broderick's success on January 7, 1898:

> In a recent conference on Christian Archaeology, held under the presidency of Cardinal (Teodolfo) Mertel, Father Bonaventure Broderick, D.D., an American priest temporarily in Rome, read a highly interesting paper on some discoveries he has made in the Roman Forum. He is a specialist in the matter of ancient inscriptions, and studies which he made of the columns in the Temple of Antonius and Faustina have permitted him

> to throw new light on the historical spot which they occupy. His discoveries included inscriptions of both pagan and Christian times, but these latter alone were important. By their aid he was able to luminously confirm the arguments already drawn from history and tradition to show that this portion of the Forum had been consecrated by the blood of the martyrs. He judged that the locality was venerated from the earliest days, and that here a sanctuary was raised, near to the site of the prefect's tribunal where so many Christians were butchered during the reign of Decius. He was further able to gather important data as to the real nature and topography of the *Locus Telluris,* the so-called temple of the earth so often mentioned in the Acts of the Martyrs.

The article closed with a radiant appraisal: "The entire paper read by Father Broderick was very highly commended by the competent persons present and is a promising indication of the brilliant future the young ecclesiastic has before him in the domain of Christian science."

The day after the flattering piece appeared in the London paper, his father died, and Bonaventure at once left Rome for his Connecticut home. Two weeks later Dr. Marucchi made international news with a discovery that Broderick told the Hartford newspaper he nearly made himself:

> Much interest has been awakened in archaeological circles by the discovery, January 24, by Professor Orazio Marucchi, Secretary of the Pontifical Archaeological Society, of a graffiti picture, or sketch, of the crucifixion of Christ, in the ruins of the palace of the Caesars on the Palatine Hill in Rome. Closely identified with this discovery is the Rev. Dr. Bonaventure F. Broderick, now in

this city, an instructor in the Catholic Seminary on Collins Street. A *Courant* reporter called upon Dr. Broderick yesterday afternoon, and he told in an interesting way his connection with the work of Professor Marucchi, with whom he has been closely related in archaeological research in Rome. Dr. Broderick, by the way, was born in Hartford and his early education was in the Parkvllle school. Since leaving here he has become a well-known student of history and archaeology, has won distinction for his scholarship and the title of "Doctor," although he is still quite a young man. "I came very near making this particular discovery myself," he said. "I have been pursuing investigations in the Forum and particularly in the palace of the Caesars just above the Forum on the Palatine Hill, paying particular attention to the graffiti, so much so that Professor Marucchi playfully calls me 'the graffiti archaeologist.' Graffiti, you must know, signifies scratches, so that the work I have been doing is deciphering, so far as possible, the scratches made upon the walls of the structures that are excavated or may be yet under the ground, as in the catacombs. I had intended to have gone through this very section of the palace to ascertain if any graffiti were there on the day of the discovery, but a cablegram came, announcing the death of my father and summoning me to America. I then turned over all the results of my investigations to Professor Marucchi. He was very anxious that I should go with him for a final visit the day before I was to leave Rome, but I was unable to do so, and he went alone. Towards evening he came to my house in an excited state of mind, greatly pleased with what he had found, indicating to me what it was, and begging me to go with him and see for myself. This I did and I am convinced that no greater discovery in archaeology has been made. Its importance cannot be exaggerated."[44]

Among the Foremost Graffitologists

Marucchi and Broderick caught the attention of Theodore Dreiser, journalist of the naturalist school who wrote that the two were "wandering through Roman ruins of all that was once magnificent" when they encountered the ancient scribblings.[45] Dreiser continued in one of his early-twentieth-century magazine articles:

> The first occasion on which the public was made acquainted with the word graffitology was when Professor Marucchi discovered the rude scratching which he took to be a first century representation of the Crucifixion. It was an uncouth piece of workmanship, but to the professor it was of utmost importance, and his theory about its origin interested the entire world.
>
> As a science, graffitology rests on the work of the gentleman named and upon that of Rev. Bonaventure F. Broderick, D.D., of the Roman Catholic seminary of Hartford, who during a period of years spent in Italy conducted investigations of the subject.[46]
>
> We must attach no more importance to the subject than is given to it by its sponsors, however Dr. Broderick believes that when studied with method, graffitology becomes one of the most interesting of the large group of historical sciences.[47]

Broderick, at age twenty-nine, had become so well known in the Christian archaeological community that he is found in the Protestant *American Journal of Theology*, mentioned in an 1898 book review of Joseph Wilpert's *Franctio Panis*, a text about the discovery of the fresco of St. Priscilla at Rome. Wilpert, an authority of catacombs and churches of ancient Rome, had been mentored by Giovanni Battista de Rossi, known for his 1849 rediscovery of the lost Catacombs of Callixtus along the Via Appia Antica. The reviewer, Charles C. Stearns, remarked,

> This book is but a fruit from the seed of the great De Rossi's incomparable preparatory labors in the field of Christian archaeology. Ere long a mass of well sifted historical facts will be forthcoming from the early Christian centuries. Another discovery, made this very winter, is warrant enough of what is certainly to come. Christian graffiti have been found in the traditional places of martyrdom near the Stadium and in the Forum, by the keen eyes of Dr. Broderick, an earnest American student.[48]

Among Father Broderick's early accomplishments is a scholarly paper, "The Burial Papers of the Jews in Ancient Rome," which was read at the Fourth International Catholic Scientific Congress at Fribourg in 1898.[49] He also began to examine the remnant of the Altar of Calvinus, the eighth century B.C. altar allegedly erected on Palatine Hill by Romulus for the ceremonial founding of Rome. Years later, he published his findings.[50]

First American Member of The Arcadia

In recognition of his contributions during his years of study in Rome, he was welcomed as a member in the centuries-old Italian literary academy *The Arcadia*,[51] the first American so honored,[52] and the *Collegium Cultorum Martyrum*,[53] established by Dr. Marucchi in 1879 to study sacred facets of the ancient world.

Years of Study Come to a Close

During his time in Rome and occasioned by his archaeological digs, he began building a collection of ancient and papal coins struck between the third century B.C. and the fourth century A.D. His vast collection, numbering seven hundred and collected between 1893 and 1898 was tucked away until 1941 when he gifted the complete collection to Manhattan College, catalogued by Frederick S. Knobloch, Fellow of the American Numismatic Society.[54]

Broderick's achievements were many during his seven years in the Eternal City, gaining on his reputation as a brilliant and multitalented scholar while winning the respect of his peers, professors, and many in the Church hierarchy.

At the same time, half a world away, civil unrest was widespread on the island of Cuba, then a colony of Spain, where Catholicism had been the state religion since the 1851 Spanish Concordat with the Vatican. The turmoil created tensions for the Church and for the United States government—tensions that would lead to the 1898 War with Spain.

The war, its aftermath, anxiety within the Church and among the hierarchy would combine to create the storm that was the complicated atmosphere in which Broderick found himself when he arrived in Cuba in 1900. These are important signs of the times that we will visit in Chapter Three, but first, his turbulent two years as a young priest in Connecticut.

2. Fast Start and First Troubles in Connecticut, 1898–1900

The Popular Young Priest at Home

After receiving news of his father's death in January of 1898 Broderick left Rome and returned to Connecticut. His outstanding academic credentials preceded his return, and he was offered a teaching position at Catholic University in Washington, but the young priest felt that as his education was paid for by the Hartford diocese it was his duty to serve in the district. On February 23, Bishop Tierney appointed him to teach at St. Thomas Seminary, the diocesan minor seminary in Hartford, founded by Tierney a year earlier.[55] Named Professor of History, Father Broderick also taught algebra, geometry, English literature, grammar, and the Italian language. In addition, he served as chaplain at the recently founded St. Francis Hospital in Hartford.[56]

At the end of the academic year, as a summer assignment, he took charge of the parish of St. Mary of the Immaculate Conception at Branford, on the shoreline forty miles south of Hartford, where the pastor, Father Edward Martin, was on a three-month sabbatical in Europe. The parish buildings were dated and inadequate and Bishop Tierney desired that a proper church be erected as soon as possible, but the aging Father Martin, in declining health, had been reluctant to begin a building project.

The young, energetic, and personable Father Broderick went fast to work and in short order proved his standing as an effective fundraiser. He found a site for a new church on the corner of Hopson Avenue and Main Street, where Dr. George Evans had previously occupied the building. He bought the property on August 12, 1898, for $10,000 and used the house as the rectory with plans to erect the new church on the adjacent lot. On August 14 he met with about one hundred men of the parish to form the St. Mary's Building Association.[57] The fundraising goal was met within five months, as reported by the *Hartford Courant*:

> When Dr. Broderick's vacation term began at the seminary where he was teaching, he was sent on an important mission to Branford by the bishop. It was desired that a church be built there, and Dr. Broderick raised $30,000. Of this amount $5,000 was given by Mr. Plant, the millionaire. Dr. Broderick was much liked by the parishioners there and the fact that he was able to raise such a large amount for the building of the church was much commended by the bishop.[58]

The generous donor named simply as "Mr. Plant, the millionaire" was Henry B. Plant, well-known and respected owner of railroads, hotels, and steamship lines, best recognized for his post-Civil War efforts in developing the southeastern United States, especially Florida. A Branford native, Plant was a Congregationalist, widowed once, whose second wife, Margaret, was Catholic and a life-long financial supporter of Church causes. Henry would die in 1899 but his widow and Broderick would remain friends until her death in 1909. We will become better acquainted with Margaret Plant in Chapter Six.

After his success in Branford, Father Broderick was sent to Westport, Connecticut in the summer of 1899 where the pastor, forty-six-year-old Father James Patrick Ryle, had taken mortally ill during the construction of a church there. Broderick took care of the weakening Father Ryle in his final months while overseeing the completion of the project.[59] The Church of the Assumption was dedicated just two weeks after Father Ryle's death.

When classes resumed at the seminary each fall Father Broderick resumed his teaching duties while also serving as a weekend assistant or acting pastor at various parishes throughout the diocese.[60]

Troubles with his Bishop

Broderick turned thirty-one in December of 1899. The following month, two years after his return from Rome, he was caught in a financial storm that implicated and embarrassed Bishop Tierney, straining their benevolent relationship to the breaking point. Newspaper accounts and Broderick's own testimony show that the controversy led Tierney to wish that the young priest would take a position in rural Connecticut, away from the limelight of Hartford.

Central to the story is Father Broderick's oldest brother Clement, the inventor, who founded and owned the Broderick Projectile Company of Windsor, Connecticut, a facility that made ammunition for the navy based in Groton, where, thirty years earlier, Connecticut donated land for the establishment of a base. Clement was the inventor of a feed for the well-known

Gatling gun.⁶¹ The navy had advertised for bids to supply 100,000 six-pound projectiles for Hotchkiss rapid-fire guns and Clement had won the $120,000 contract. To meet production requirements Clement leased the former Spencer Automatic Machine Screw factory⁶² and in 1898 the factory was running night and day under the supervision of David Broderick, who had returned from Germany to help his brother.

Clement also discovered a way to make percussion fuses for the shells at a lower rate than all earlier contractors and secured a second contract for 200,000 of these devices.⁶³ He estimated it would take sixteen months of night and day work to fulfill the contract.⁶⁴

The increase in manufacturing activity required more capital and Clement, having little, was helped by several investors including his priest brother, who took a loan for $12,000. Years later Bonaventure claimed that it was Father William Redding of Unionville who came to him and convinced him he should finance the business for his brother.⁶⁵ In 1899 something soured the relationship, and the factory was closed for three weeks. "Differences between the three brothers caused most of the trouble," the Hartford *Courant* reported.

> Clement makes charges against his two brothers, and they have their counter charges. The factory was closed about three weeks ago. It was evident that the work could not continue without more capital, as Clement was unable to meet the notes for borrowed money as they fell due, and a halt was called. Those who have loaned money to Clement were willing to let their money remain provided he would give them a good endorser on his notes to them. Mr. Broderick was unable

to do this until Saturday. He now claims that this matter has been settled and that business at the factory will start up today.[66]

The "good endorser" of the notes was Bishop Tierney. According to Bonaventure, Father Redding told him that Bishop Tierney would endorse a note for $10,000 if Clement would get his life insured for that sum to secure the bishop. Bonaventure argued that his brother was in poor health[67] and not insurable. It was at the suggestion of Father Redding, Bonaventure recalled, that he took a policy out on his own life and Bishop Tierney then endorsed the note. Even after an infusion of cash, the business continued to struggle and to save his $10,000 Bishop Tierney put in another $5,000. Soon the business was an absolute failure, and all was lost.[68]

It was front-page news when the factory failed. The article that hurt Bishop Tierney most was headlined "This Bishop Makes Bombs."[69] He talked to Bonaventure about the matter and wanted him to quietly leave Hartford for a church 100 miles to the southwest in Stamford, a city half the size of Hartford, with a population of less than 20,000. The young priest objected, saying he did not want to be made a scapegoat as he had not intentionally done anything wrong. Tierney then asked the rector of the seminary to speak with Bonaventure. Because of what the rector said, Bonaventure took all his belongings from his residence at the seminary and moved to his brother David's house.

Two days later Tierney sent for him. They talked the matter over. He told Tierney again that he did not want to be seen as a scapegoat by leaving Hartford and that he did not like the way the rector had talked to him. Tierney told him that the rector, in talking the way he did, exceeded his authority and Bonaventure was not to blame.

The bishop decided to send him to Westport where the pastor had taken ill. Father Broderick went to Westport, a town of 4,000, twenty miles shy of Stamford, with mixed emotions: he had that same sense of loyalty with which he declined the Catholic University offer a year earlier, that it was his duty to serve in the diocese, however, this time the chaos created by Clement's failed business venture made this awkward. What to do? He decided to discuss his predicament with the papal legation at Washington, D.C.[70]

The Answer to his Troubles

His February 1900 visit to Washington resulted in two job offers. One, the teaching position at Catholic University was still available to him, but he may have wondered if it would still appear he was running from the troubles at home. The second offer was one that was a great distance from Hartford and a clear advancement, giving him a greater level of comfort regarding appearances.[71]

That offer came from his former professor, Donato Sbarretti,[72] who, the previous month, had been named Bishop of Havana. Sbarretti had been an auditor with the Apostolic Delegation in Washington since 1893. After seven years in the U.S. Sbarretti knew well the landscape of the Church in America, but he also knew his limitations, and knew he needed an American secretary talented in social and diplomatic circles. He turned to his former student. The opportunity to go to Cuba with his erstwhile professor was now on the table; the timing was extraordinary, and it was a fortunate arrangement, for one personality balanced the other. Author Brendan Finn, who became a Broderick friend late in the bishop's life, commented on their complementary natures:

> Bishop Sbarretti, though lacking in the social graces, had a thorough knowledge of the workings of the Roman Curia and an equally extensive acquaintance with American affairs, both ecclesiastical and political. Broderick, on the other hand, possessed the natural warmth and cordiality of the Gael, coupled with the shrewdness of the typical New England Yankee.[73]

He accepted Sbaretti's offer and was granted a two-year leave of absence from a relieved Bishop Tierney, but the embarrassment of Clement's business failure did not end quietly. Days before he shipped off to Cuba, he was sued by the Geometric Drill Co. for one of Clement's outstanding bills. The New Haven, Connecticut *Morning Journal-Courier* reported the lawsuit under the headline, "Pastor Sued." [74] And later the Waterbury *Evening Democrat* reported "By consent of counsel on both sides of the lawsuit of the Holmes, Booth & Hayden company against Bonaventure Broderick, judgment was given today for $3,164.74. This was a suit to recover on a note."[75]

With all the bad press he may have appeared to some as a man on the run, but with the troubles of Connecticut behind him, he seemed to have been energized when, on the brink of a new century, he arrived in Cuba in the spring of 1900.

It was a fresh start for the young priest, but it was a season complicated by the aftermath of the War with Spain, a season better appreciated with an overview of the War and its aftermath.

3. The War with Spain

Father Broderick and Bishop Sbarretti arrived in Cuba thirteen months after the short-lived conflict. America's War with Spain involved Cuba, the Philippines, Guam, and Puerto Rico. On the Cuban front the battle was preceded by decades of domestic hostility fostered by revolutionaries seeking freedom from Spain's colonial rule.

The four-century history of Cuba as a colony of Spain is complex and has been recorded widely. To summarize, the latter half of the nineteenth century saw uprisings among Cuban-born citizens seeking independence, first leading to the "Ten Years War" from 1868-1878, followed a year later by the "Little War" for independence that was soon squashed by the Spaniards, who kept control; and although a truce followed for many years, economic and social problems persisted.

While Broderick was studying in Rome the political situation in Cuba was deteriorating. Civil unrest escalated in 1895 leading to a war for independence. Both the United States and Vatican were concerned for a variety of reasons, among them, for the United States, commerce, and for the Vatican, the Spanish government's enormous financial support to the Church in Cuba. President Grover Cleveland insisted on neutrality, while the Vatican tried to keep the peace by recruiting Archbishop John Ireland,[76] the politically astute and articulate bishop of St. Paul, Minnesota, to engage with the administration of Cleveland's successor, William McKinley, elected in 1896. Ireland undertook the task reluctantly, apprehensive that accusations of papal interference would embolden Americans already infected with anti-Catholic tendencies.[77] The Vatican attempt at peace failed, and the revolution drew a heavy-handed Spanish response.

"The Butcher" Returns

The oppression began in earnest in February 1896 with the arrival from Spain of General Valeriano Weyler, son of a German father and Spanish mother. Nicknamed "The Butcher" and called "the prince of all cruel generals," Weyler had been sent to the island once before, during the Ten Years War. *The Times* of Philadelphia painted a graphic picture of what his return to Cuba would mean: "There is nothing to prevent his carnal, animal brain from running riot with itself in inventing tortures and infamies of bloody debauchery, which he will dignify under the comprehensive title of martial law."[78]

Ohio's John Sherman took to the floor of the U.S. Senate to prophesy the atrocities that Weyler's return would bring. "This man Weyler is one of worst men which could have been sent to a pacific people. Warfare massacre. He openly avows it. He is a brute, pure and simple, and his hands are stained with blood of defenseless men and women."[79]

> In support of this statement, Mr. Sherman sent to the desk and had extracts which were most startling and sensational. They recited the atrocities of Weyler's former command in Cuba which sent a murmur of horror through the crowded galleries. One of the statements was that Gen. Weyler had captured parents and their several daughters, pretty senoritas. He ordered the young

girls stripped naked and then compelled them to dance, thus naked, before the Spanish troops, while the parents were driven to the point of insanity. But this was not all. Mr. Sherman interrupted at this point and asked that the recital be suspended. The senator went on with extracts from recent interviews with Weyler, in which he spoke of exterminating the Cubans.[80]

"These showed him to be," said Sherman, "a demon rather than a general." The senator added, "if this continues no earthly power can prevent the people of the United States from going to that island, sweeping over it from end to end and driving out these barbarians. I share in the responsibility of the course we must take," said Sherman in closing, "confident in the justice of this course, confident the justice of the Almighty ruler the universe, and I feel that we should aid in securing for Cuba the same liberty we now enjoy."[81]

Weyler's unspeakable cruelty began to peak on October 21, 1896, one month before William McKinley's election as U.S. President, when the Spaniard ordered Cubans in rural areas to move into reconcentration areas in fortified towns where food and medical supplies were soon insufficient. By the following May news of the mounting atrocities was on front pages nationwide. "The accounts are harrowing, are horrifying," reported the Wilmington *Messenger*. The Baltimore *Herald* stated, Weyler "has not only removed women and children, old men, and boys from their homes in the country to the cities but has huddled them together there without any provision for feeding them. To put the matter mildly, it amounts to a war of extermination upon peaceful and defenseless people. It is no more a necessity of war than wholesale murder is, and reliable newspaper correspondents for months have denounced the policy as an outrage against humanity."[82]

Public sympathy for the rebels began to swell among Catholics and Protestants alike, but what were Americans to make of the call by Sherman and others for the U.S. to respond with force? Catholics in the states, unlike those in Spain, were used to a separation of state powers from church powers, and many Catholics harbored the thought that military intervention by the United States, even on behalf of the Cuban revolutionaries, would seem like a war on the Catholicism of Spain. But those Catholics were also Americans, and many were proud immigrants.

Historian Frank T. Reuter sets the stage in *Catholic Influence on American Colonial Polices, 1898-1904:*

> A new spirit of growth and change were pervading the country, shaking off the lethargy left in the wake of the Civil War. A demand for greater industrial expansion, overseas markets, and international commerce was a part of this spirit. A war against the decaying empire of Spain might fulfill this demand and set the United States on the road toward future greatness. To the expansionist minded American, Spain stood in the way of this future. The destruction of Spanish power would mean new American opportunities in Cuba, in the long desired isthmian canal, and perhaps even in the Philippines.[83]

Still, there were rumblings in the Protestant press having elements of anti-Catholicism in condemning Spanish policies and subtle inferences that Catholics could not be loyal citizens if the United States entered the fray. These charges were not new; the bishops of the United States earlier refuted accusations of a double allegiance in a pastoral letter issued by the Third Plenary Council of Baltimore (December 7, 1884):

> We repudiate with equal earnestness the assertion that we need to lay aside any of our devotedness to our Church to be true Americans; the insinuation that we need to abate any of our love for our country's principles and institutions to be faithful Catholics. To argue that the Catholic Church is hostile to our great republic, because she teaches that "there is no power but from God" (John 8:32); because, therefore back of the events which led to the formation of the republic, she sees the providence of God leading to that issue, and back of our Country's laws the authority of God as their sanction— this is evidently so illogical and contradictory an accusation, that we are astonished to hear it advanced by persons of ordinary intelligence. We believe that our country's heroes were the instruments of the God of Nations in establishing this home of freedom; to both the Almighty and to His instruments in the work, we look with grateful reverence; and to maintain the inheritance of freedom which they have left us, should it ever — which God forbid — be imperiled, our Catholic citizens will be found to stand forward, as one man ready to pledge anew "their lives, their fortunes, and their sacred honor."[84]

In early 1897, Catholics and Protestants alike were still asking: Was Weyler as cruel as the press and Senator Sherman portrayed? "Weyler is really the monster described by the American press. His crimes against humanity dishonor my country," said a man identified as Senor Barroeta, a former captain in the Spanish army and owner of a Spanish newspaper in Cienfuegos who could not stand the general's barbarity and dishonesty. "The civil guard tortures the prisoners to extort confessions from them. Weyler has ordered the concentration in the towns of the country people. He aims to depopulate the island. The general's only aim is naturally to continue in office where he gratifies his natural cruelty and ambition."[85]

As 1897 dragged on in Cuba, with atrocities mounting and the Vatican desperately seeking a peaceful resolution, clamoring for U.S. intervention was on the rise in the American press. "If the American Eagle ever gave one scream over Cuba, Butcher Weyler would fall off the earth," proclaimed the *Shreveport Weekly Journal*.[86] Another journalist favoring intervention claimed that without it the war would continue until all Cubans were dead, because nothing less would satisfy "the thirst for blood inherent in the bull-fighting citizens of Spain."[87]

Theodore Roosevelt, who, in a few short years, as President, would become an ally of Bishop Broderick, wrote as then-Assistant Secretary of the Navy, that "intervention would be as righteous as advantageous."[88]

The Battleship Maine *Is Sunk*

Still, the McKinley administration remained reluctant to interfere; that is, until February 15, 1898, when a mysterious explosion sunk the American battleship *Maine* in the Havana harbor killing 260 American sailors. The *Catholic Telegraph* claimed 190 crew members of the Maine were Roman Catholic. One of the survivors was Father John P. Chidwick, the chaplain and a priest of the Boston diocese where *The Pilot*, Boston's Catholic newspaper, recalling a national hero of the War of 1812, demanded President McKinley "display a tithe of the resolution which Andrew Jackson would have shown in a similar crisis."[89]

Roosevelt, in writing to a friend, Brooks Adams, declared "The blood of the Cubans, the blood of women and children who have perished by the hundred thousand in hideous misery, lies at our door; and the blood of the murdered men of the *Maine* calls not for indemnity but for the full measure of atonement which can only come by driving the Spaniard from the new world."[90]

It was the *Maine* tragedy and its fallout that at last prompted McKinley's request of Congress "for authorization to end the fighting in Cuba between the rebels and Spanish forces, and to establish a 'stable government' that would 'maintain order' and ensure the 'peace and tranquility and the security' of Cuban and U.S. citizens on the island."[91]

War in Cuba came and lasted less than four months (April 21–August 13, 1898). Diplomat John Hay has been credited with coining the phrase describing the conflict as "a splendid little war" but the battles that spread beyond Cuba had cost more than four thousand American lives between 1898 and 1902.

The successful effort to free Cuba paid a dividend when navy vessels commanded by George Dewey destroyed the Spanish fleet in Manila's harbor in the Philippines. As Reuter observed, "the dream of an American overseas empire suddenly seemed near fulfillment. What had been originally a war of liberation in Cuba now became a war of acquisition in the Pacific and the Caribbean."[92]

The Treaty of Paris of 1898 officially ended the war on December 10, when Spain agreed to grant independence to Cuba, cede Guam and Puerto Rico to the United States and sell the

Philippines to the United States for $20 million, but hostilities soon erupted in the Philippines extending the fighting into 1902. In the end, the final American victory brought to a close Spain's colonial empire in the Western Hemisphere.

Avenues of commerce had been open between the states and Cuba before the war, principally in the market for sugar produced on the island, but the American victory, as predicted by Roosevelt's "advantageous" comment, helped many U.S. businesses, especially those in construction. Cuba's infrastructure was primitive, riddled by years of violence, and in dire need of modernization. The island's water and sewer systems, or often lack thereof, led to deadly wide-spread outbreaks of yellow fever.

Those concerns were beyond the purview of Sbarretti and Broderick. They were facing the daunting task of negotiating the settlement of Church property, a challenging mission that would require the collaboration of a trifecta of American occupation leaders, Church hierarchy, and Cuban politicians. Jose M. Hernandez, author, and professor of history, describes the political scene facing the bishop and his secretary:

> The bishops of the Cuban Church as well as many priests identified themselves totally with the Spanish side during the war, at war's end the Church was politically discredited as an institution. It had reached the nadir of its prestige. In 1898 consequently there was only one political force still operative on the Cuban scene, and that was that of the partisans of independence, of whom the most compact and substantial component was the liberating army. When Washington entered the Cuban struggle for independence and eventually destroyed the rebel military organization and the institutions it had created, Cuba became a *tabula rasa* politically once more.[93]

By the time Broderick arrived the political environment was ripe for resentment, rumor, and revenge. His skill at relationship-building and in financial matters was on full display, first as secretary to Sbarretti, and later as auxiliary bishop. It seemed to Sbarretti that he picked the right man for the job, but others higher up would later have their doubts.

Not only was the political environment in disarray but the entire nation was falling apart, best illustrated by the comments of Major General William Ludlow, Chief Engineer of the armies in the field:

> You must admit, however, that the city of Havana is in a deplorable condition. The Spaniards have left it bankrupt, unable to pay its employees, who have lacked their salaries for many months. The prisons, asylums, and homes for the destitute are without supplies, food, or medicine. The sanitary condition is frightful. Almost inconceivable abuses exist, which are a continuing menace to the health of the city. The Spaniards have left Havana with scarcely an attribute of modern civilization and practically in the sanitary condition of a city of two centuries ago.[94]

If Havana was as Ludlow described, the conditions of the rest of the island can only be imagined. Broderick was concerned for the pastoral care of Cubans living under these conditions but as priest and later bishop, was in no position to effect changes in the infrastructure. The irony is that less than ten years later he would be the majority owner of a company building a multi-million-dollar sewer system in Cienfuegos, on the southern coast.

With this background, we return to our man in Havana.

4. Cuba and the Road to the Episcopacy, 1900–1903

On January 15, 1900, as Father Broderick was suffering the consequences from brother Clement's failed business venture, Donato Sbarretti, the newly appointed Bishop of Havana asked him to become his American secretary in Cuba,[95] thus solving the conflict between Bishop Tierney and Broderick by driving a 1,500-mile wedge between the two.

During the transition period, in a move to accommodate sea travel from the states to and from Cuba and Rome, Father Broderick purchased a home and moved his mother from Connecticut to 2 Tower Place, a home directly across the street from the Monastery Church of the Sacred Heart in Yonkers. During the several years that followed Margaret Broderick was healthy enough to travel often to both Havana and Rome with her son.

Three Years as the American Secretary

Sbarretti and Broderick arrived in Havana early in 1900 during the period of U.S. military rule of the island, a time that officially began January 1, 1899, and ended with formal Cuban independence May 1, 1902. It was a time that required Church leaders to be deeply involved in affairs of state.

Sbarretti was replacing the Spanish-born Manuel Santander who, according to the press, resigned "because he could not bring himself into sympathy with the new order of things in Cuba."[96] This new order of things was the result of the emancipation of the island from Spain and its government, a government whose rich support of the Church on the island evaporated overnight.

Santander resigned in November of 1899, after twelve years at the helm. Much to the chagrin of Cuban Catholics one of their own was not chosen to replace him; instead the Italian-born Sbarretti was appointed. The *Times-Democrat* of New Orleans ran an article headlined "Bitter Opposition to Sbarretti in Cuba," but the new bishop and his secretary were up to the task; as author Brendan Finn noted years later, "Few Americans, indeed few Catholics, have an adequate idea of the triumph achieved by Bishop Sbarretti and Father Broderick in Cuba."[97]

Santander had dealt with many problems, several festering for years, including debates over civil marriage and divorce, and controversies surrounding public education. To this list were now added the problems of fiscal strain resulting from the loss of Spain's financial backing, and control of the vast church properties throughout the island. These burdens now fell to Sbarretti and Broderick, and they dealt with each successfully. The top priority, and the most complicated, was the settlement of church property.[98] Broderick would later lament that his duties were mostly administrative, though he did at times minister to those suffering from leprosy or yellow fever,[99] and was responsible for bringing religious sisters to the island to teach, including the Sisters of Providence from Baltimore and the Dominican Sisters from Albany.[100]

Prior to the nineteenth century, there was little controversy on the island over real estate, but in 1841, the governor, Jeronimo Valdes, began seizing property including that of the monastic orders, diverting it to the use of the government, during which time Spain paid the Church large sums of money for its maintenance. The seizures in question after the war included the friary of the Franciscans, which was being used as the Custom House; the convent of the Dominicans, used by the national university; the convent of the Augustinians, used by the Academy of Sciences; and the convent of San Ysidro, previously used by the Spaniards as military barracks.[101]

All these properties, and others that were held by the Church before Valdes, became subject to negotiation between the government and the Vatican with Sbarretti and Broderick on the ground in Cuba. Adding to the difficulty were the mortgages still held by Spain against property once given to the Church for its use but later taken over by the government for its own purposes.[102]

After the war, all financial support of Spain for the Church in Cuba came to a crashing halt, and the American government, in occupying the island, began to use the properties for the same administrative purposes as had Spain's government. The Church, in claiming its rights to the property, relied on Broderick and Sbarretti to negotiate all these details with the Cubans and a judicial commission set up by the U.S. government.

These negotiations required Sbarretti and Broderick to deal directly with Major General John R. Brooke, the first military governor, and later, the second military governor, General Leonard Wood, and Placide Louis Chapelle, Archbishop of

New Orleans, the Apostolic Delegate to Cuba and the Philippines.

Before his resignation as Bishop of Havana Santander told newspapers, "Although it seems that Archbishop Chapelle is in harmony with the administration at Washington, yet his views in regard to the holding of ecclesiastical property seem to be at variance with those of the officials in the islands."[103] In time, Broderick would have his own major conflict with Chapelle, a skirmish that would lead to his undoing in Cuba.

The church properties in question were vast, and ownership complicated, but time was of the essence. Both Washington and Rome wanted all claims settled while Cuba was governed by the United States, before native rule was formally established as expected in 1902. The complexity of the situation, the need to recover property and generate revenue for the church was outlined by the *Atlanta Constitution* on July 7, 1901:

> The property question between the church and the military government in Cuba is very little understood. Many times, the statement has been made that Bishop Sbarretti occupied a major part of his time in endeavoring to enforce the right of the church to a large amount of real estate and census property which had been fraudulently claimed by his predecessor, this property in reality being the property of the municipality held by Spanish authorities who, when defeat was inevitable, had it falsely recorded as church property. This statement is entirely false and under conditions as they really exist it was no heinous offense for Bishop Sbarretti to make strenuous efforts to have property restored rightfully belonging to the church. The financial condition of the church in the island is very deplorable. The bishop took possession

of his see with an exhausted treasury with parishes all over the land begging aid, the convents, and other religious institutions without means of support looking to the church in Havana for the wherewithal upon which to live. Many priests on the island were serving without pay and they in many instances suffered for common necessities. The bishop has even been compelled to borrow largely in order to partially meet the demands from all sections.

The harm caused to the church in Cuba by its loss of financial support of Spain cannot be overstated. The *American Catholic Quarterly Review* noted that the government of Spain compensated the Church in Cuba $403,149 in one year alone (1896) for government use of Church property.[104] The sudden loss of this revenue presented a huge obstacle for the new bishop and his secretary.

This upheaval, coupled with that of the body politic, made for a volatile atmosphere where, successes aside, a disaster of some sort was inevitable.

Broderick was tasked with planning and conducting all negotiations for settling the property question.[105] Forgoing burdensome detail, suffice to say that he and Sbarretti in one year had accomplished to the satisfaction of all, including Chapelle, everything that the Church expected regarding the retrieval of, or just compensation for, its property located in the diocese.

Broderick, "the Connecticut Yankee who was fighting for the existence of the Church in Cuba," [106] had developed a close working relationship with Governor General Wood, "the Cape Cod Yankee who rose to high military rank and fame."[107] He presented Wood with a list of properties claimed by the Church, and after negotiations, a multi-million-dollar settlement was reached.[108]

The *Boston Globe* weighed in on their success:

> With the advent of the American occupation the payment of the budget of public worship ceased, but the intervening government still held possession and administration of ecclesiastical property. The church was confronted with the twofold question: First to settle accounts with the state, and second, to adjust itself to the new conditions. In the meantime, the Holy See had appointed an apostolic delegate to Cuba, Most Rev. Archbishop Chapelle, and the first case of the delegate was based upon the dictates of equity and the guarantee of the treaty of Paris to recover the administration of said property. Before leaving for the Philippines in December 1899, where the crisis in church affairs had hurriedly summoned him, negotiations looking to that end were initiated by the apostolic delegate with the authorities in Washington and were in a masterly manner carried out and brought to a satisfactory conclusion by Bishop Sbarretti and Rev. Dr. Broderick on behalf of the church and Gen. Leonard Wood, representing the government of the United States. In consequence of the separation of church and state the purpose of the holy see, through the apostolic delegate, has been to place the external administration of church affairs on a footing similar to that which exists in the United States and the British empire.[109]

The Philippines are Considered

In the meantime, trouble was brewing for Chapelle who was struggling with his responsibilities in the Philippines. He was unable to gain cooperation from the monastic orders there[110] and was often at odds with William Howard Taft, the governor general of the Philippines.[111] Taft finally let the Vatican know that Chapelle had overstayed his usefulness and he was recalled in the summer of 1901.

Broderick knew a change was afoot and, anticipating that he would be sent to the Philippines, a great distance from New York, he became concerned for his mother's well-being and care. He went to St. Louis in July of 1901 to the convent of the Sisters of the Good Shepherd, where it is thought he sought permission for, or at least discussed the possibility of, a nun by the name of Sr. Mary of St. Helena, to care for his mother. The following November, Miss Helen Bowlen moved into the Yonkers household as a companion and caregiver to Margaret Broderick.[112] Much more is said of Miss Bowlen in later chapters.

The proposed change in the Philippines involved Sbarretti, who had proven himself as bishop in Cuba. On September 16, 1901, he was appointed Apostolic Delegate to the Philippines to replace Chapelle and asked Broderick to go with him. Broderick agreed and would later claim that at the time he chose to decline an appointment to become bishop of Havana, so motivated was he to remain with Sbarretti.[113] Indeed, that would be the first of two times he refused to be a candidate for the bishopric, the second, the summer of 1902, when the elevation was proposed by Archbishop Chapelle.[114]

Monsignor Broderick

Broderick was invited to Rome, and on November 30, 1901, Pope Leo XIII, in a private audience, praised him for his work in connection with the property question in Cuba, and at the same time named him a papal chamberlain, giving him the title "Monsignor."[115] The Naugatuck, Connecticut, *Daily News* reported on the event:

> The friends of the Rev. Dr. Bonaventure Broderick will be pleased to learn that on the recommendation of Archbishop Sbaretti, he has been appointed an honorary chamberlain to the Pope, with the title of monsignor. The dignity of monsignor carries with it the title of "right reverend," and gives the person the right to wear Episcopal purple. Monsignor Broderick has been, for some time, secretary to Archbishop Sbaretti in Havana and the new dignity has been conferred upon him to mark the Pope's appreciation of the fact and diplomatic skill with which he has performed his secretarial duties. Archbishop Sbaretti has been appointed apostolic delegate to Manila and Monsignor Broderick will continue to be associated with him as secretary. The archbishop and the monsignor became acquainted some years ago, when Dr. Broderick was a talented student in Rome and Dr. Sbaretti, a professor in the college. The dispatch which announces the promotion of Monsignor Broderick states that he will visit his relatives in New England before he takes his departure for the Philippines, which will be the field of his future work.[116]

The Philippines Reconsidered

The proposed transition of the team to the Philippines caused William Henry Thorne, publisher, and editor of *The Globe: A New Review of World Literature, Society, Religion, Art, and Politics*, to revive the memory of Clement Broderick's failed projectile business:

It is announced too, that Rev. Bonaventure F. Broderick, D.D., formerly located in the Diocese of Hartford, Conn., and who since a not forgotten episode in that diocese has been with Mgr. Sbarretti and during the past two years acting as his private secretary, will accompany the Monsignor in his mission as Apostolic Delegate to the Philippines.[117]

The same issue of *The Globe* highlighted Chapelle's failure in Manila while casting doubt that Sbarretti would, in the end, succeed him. The publication claimed that replacing Chappelle "would further the truth of the current rumor that the archbishop's mission to Manila was not wholly successful." The article carried the caveat that Broderick would accompany Sbarretti to Manila "that is, if Sbarretti becomes the delegate. On his arrival at New York, it is known, a letter ordering him not to proceed to Washington but at once to return to Rome, hurried him off on the next Transatlantic steamer."[118]

The analysis of *The Globe* was prophetic: Sbarretti never made it to the Philippines. When he returned to Rome, he learned that he was recalled by the Vatican because his appointment was not accepted by Taft who, for reasons unknown, disliked Sbarretti.[119] Instead, he was sent to Canada and Newfoundland as apostolic delegate and Giovanni Baptiste Guidi was sent to Manila as Chapelle's replacement.

Broderick remained in New York while Sbarretti made haste back to Rome. He soon received a telegram calling him to Cuba to help settle properties in the Santiago diocese. He told of the trip in a letter written to his friend and former Rector at the North American College, Monsignor Denis J. O'Connell, by now Rector of the Catholic University of America in Washington:

> The archbishop (of Santiago) telegraphed me that it was absolutely necessary for me to come to Havana as Gen. Wood had not done anything toward reaching a settlement. I reached Havana on the 6th of Jan. and on the 11th, we signed the agreement between Gen. Wood and the archbishop.
>
> This agreement returned to the church or brought from it $610,000 worth of its property which had been held by the Government. Both the Governor General and the Archbishop were pleased with the arrangement. The General and Mrs. Wood gave me a dinner on the night of the 11th and the archbishop on the 13th.
>
> As I was leaving in the morning of the 14th the archbishop handed me a thousand dollars to bring to my mother, so pleased was he with what I had done for him.[120]

In the same letter he hints at a clash between his friend Sbarretti and Archbishop Ireland: "I am glad to hear that (Sbarretti) is prospering. He is wise ... and when the opportunity comes will not forget the *maleato* Ireland made him face during the journey from New York to Rome." What the hammering was that Sbarretti had to endure from Ireland is not known.

Within weeks of writing the letter to O'Connell from New York, Broderick, now a monsignor, returned to Havana, selected by Leo XIII to be the official representative of the Church at the Inauguration of the Republic of Cuba on May 20, 1902. For the next year he labored in Cuba as the American secretary while Havana remained without a resident bishop.

David Broderick in Cuba

During this period, the post-war reconstruction of Cuba was in full swing. American know-how and goods were in great demand. After the failure of brother Clement's ammunition manufacturing business, David Broderick went into business as a manufacturer's representative. Several companies from his hometown were active in Cuba and all were represented by David, who "was instrumental in securing the necessary contracts with the American government for these small town, family operated Unionville businesses. David Broderick was not involved in any one industry. He acted rather as an agent for all the Unionville companies present in Havana."[121]

Unionville, according to one account, was so named because it joined the corners of Farmington, Burlington, and Avon. In 1900 the population was about 6,000[122] and there were many businesses in addition to the Unionville paper mills. The largest employer was the Upson Nut Company, which exported wood planes, nuts and bolts, rules, and levels. Other companies manufactured rivets, cutlery, rat traps, gunstocks, mining knives, glass cutters, scrapers, and ball bearings, all useful items in the reconstruction effort in Cuba.[123] David's success led many to suspect that his priest brother was using his influential position to direct contracts his way.

Friends in High Places

Monsignor Broderick was making friends in high places—outside the Church—not only in industry, but in government, both Cuban and American. Chief among those political friendships were Pablo Desvernine, then Minister of Finance for Cuba; U.S. Senator Mark Hanna of Ohio; and Elihu Root, who served in President McKinley's cabinet, and later, that of Theodore Roosevelt.

Bishop Broderick

The following year was bittersweet for the Broderick family. Clement, 37, who was said to be in ill health during the 1900 bomb-building factory debacle, died of heart disease at his home in Hartford in the afternoon of Friday, July 18, leaving his wife, Mary, and five young children. His obituary in the Hartford paper reported "His mother is with Mgr. Broderick in Havana, and it is thought possible that they may be able to reach here for the funeral."[124] It appears they were not able to return in time as the funeral Mass was celebrated by Father F. J. Carroll early Monday morning, July 21.[125]

Two months later, on September 16, Bonaventure was appointed Auxiliary Bishop of San Cristobal de la Habana and Titular Bishop of Juliopolis.[126] The *Boston Globe* carried a flattering commentary:

> He has the honor of being the youngest American clergyman wearing a mitre. His nomination has been enthusiastically received by all classes. Msgr. Broderick, although young in years, has had a wide experience in the management of affairs. He is learned, zealous, prudent, full of energy and practical. The apostolic delegate, as well as the clergy and people of Cuba, are satisfied that Msgr. Broderick will render eminent services. He is an American, but no one takes a truer and deeper interest in the welfare of the Cuban people than he.[127]

The latter title, that of Titular Bishop of Juliopolis,[128] he continued to embrace in the long years of exile that followed later:

"Once a bishop in the Catholic church, always a bishop" he would declare from the witness stand in a 1913 courtroom appearance.[129]

A "triple consecration" followed in Havana's cathedral on October 28, 1903, that included Broderick and two native Cubans: Havana's new bishop Pedro Gonzales Estrada, and the new bishop of Pinar del Rio, Manuel Orne. President Palma and key members of the diplomatic corps were present to witness what the *Catholic News* of New York called an "important epoch in the reorganization of the Catholic Church in Cuba."[130] The principal consecrator was Archbishop Chapelle.

In Bishop Broderick's own words, he now "had full charge of all the diplomatic, legal, business, welfare and social work of the Church in the island."[131]

No one foresaw the storm clouds gathering on the horizon. Soon, Archbishop Chapelle, in Broderick's view, began to persecute him atrociously,[132] and before the end of the next year travelled to the Vatican to level the damning charges against Bishop Broderick.

What went wrong?

5. Rumors and the Grave Misunderstanding, 1904–1905

Among the congratulatory letters the newly consecrated bishop received, several reveal his close friendships and confidences: one is worth examining, that of fifty-nine-year-old Elihu Root. In 1899 President McKinley selected Root to serve as Secretary of War, a position he continued to hold until 1903 in the cabinet of Theodore Roosevelt, McKinley's successor following his assassination. A lawyer, Root returned to private practice in 1904. He wrote to Broderick on April 28 from Pasadena, California[133] where he was taking a respite for health reasons. The candid letter betrays Root's trust in Broderick. He speaks of several personalities they both knew well, including the late Ohio Senator Mark Hanna, and 1904 presidential hopefuls, Alton Parker, Grover Cleveland, and William Randolph Hearst. Root does not hold back his feelings toward two others: Theodore Roosevelt and General Leonard Wood. Broderick has an agreeable relationship with both despite the negative tone Root takes.

> I haven't written you since you were consecrated to your present high position. How do you like wearing the purple and being a real Bishop? Mrs. Root and I would like to see you in your robes saying mass—is that properly put?—in the Cathedral. Do you find the Cubans inimical to you these days? You used to have a lot of

palaver that kept them smoothed down but now that they are getting used to playing alone maybe they are more cocky. Write me and tell me all about yourself.

Like the rest of the old guard, you must have followed the fight against Wood's confirmation in the Senate with great interest. It simply enrages me every time I think of that lying rascal, devoid of honor, being where he is. Had Hanna lived there might have been a chance to beat him, but he was born under a lucky star and when the Ohio leader died, it was all over.

I know you felt a sense of personal loss at the death of the Senator. He was a fine man and I was vainly hoping that he might get the nomination away from Roosevelt when the end came. Teddy really makes me sick. His cheap moralizing and his assumption that he is pretty near the whole Government give me a pain and I won't vote for him, even if I get a chance. I'd like to see Cleveland put up but I'm afraid there is no chance. It looks very much like Parker, doesn't it? Isn't Willie Hearst a fine campaign joke?

I suppose that you get to New York every now and then. I'm sure I should like to see you and talk over old times. There's no telling when I'll see you again. My health is steadily improving but of course it is a hard fight. I have been out here almost a year now and the chances are I shall have to stay another year. I have got almost over the fever stage now and while I'm not strong enough to do much I'm perfectly comfortable and enjoy life.

Root wrote of his friendship with John Barry Ryan, son of Thomas Fortune Ryan, wealthy New York banker and financier. Noting that young Ryan is a great fellow whose eight-year marriage has produced five children, Root exclaims "There isn't much danger of the heretics outnumbering the faithful while he is around."

He inquired of Margaret Plant, the Catholic benefactor from Branford and remarried widow of Henry B. Plant. "Was it a shock to you that Mrs. Plant married Bobbie Graves? If I remember correctly, she was a great friend of yours in your younger days. Graves is a very fine-looking man but a divorce (sic) I believe and therefore, I presume, in your official black books."

In closing he wrote, "Give my regards to Joe if he is still in Havana and the rest of the bunch, including the two Judges—Big and Little, and old Steinhart. Don't fail to write me." Who the judges were is not known, but the reference to "old Steinhart" is to Frank Steinhart, a political figure who played a prominent role in Broderick's later legal problems.

The following year, Root's health improved as well as his attitude toward Roosevelt: he returned to Washington and accepted the president's invitation to rejoin his cabinet as Secretary of State.

From his first day in Cuba in 1900 as Sbarretti's secretary Broderick was in position to make the acquaintance of a great many influential people like Root, as well as Cuban politicians, businessmen with interests on the island, and Wall Street executives such as the officers of Coudert Brothers international banking firm, who handled the financial transactions involving church property. These relationships were vital to exercising his responsibilities and served him well at the time. Regrettably, some would later cause him great difficulty, legal and otherwise, always involving money. "I know that Wall Street always had a fascination for him. In fact, it was the beginning of his troubles," a fellow prelate would write years later.[134]

His Circle in Cuba

Among those in Broderick's circle we find Hugh J. Reilly, Sr., a businessman from Boston who called on Broderick with letters of introduction from John D. Crimmins, prominent New York City contractor, philanthropist and supporter of Irish American and Roman Catholic concerns; John A. Sullivan, a member of Congress from Massachusetts; William Sulzer, a congressman and future governor of New York; Juan Antonio Frias, once a Cuban senator and mayor of Cienfuegos; and Frank Steinhart, who served as Consul General for a period of time. We will meet these gentlemen again a few years later in the legal drama that unfolds in Chapter Eight.

Add to this list the bishop's brother, David, who, as he continued to represent Connecticut businesses in Cuba, was securing profitable contracts with the government.[135] Suspicions of influence by Bonaventure, now a bishop, began to surface more frequently.

Broderick was popular and well-liked on the island, and during the three years before becoming bishop had earned the respect of many. Chief among his native Cuban admirers was Pablo Desvernine y Galdós. Desvernine was a member of a family whose real estate holdings on the island were likened by the *Wall Street Journal* to those of the Astors in New York. Educated in the U.S. at Columbia College, Desvernine was a lawyer and representative of the Bank of Cuba. In 1899 he was named Secretary of Finance in the cabinet of General Brooke, the immediate military governor following the war.[136] He would later hold other prominent positions as a diplomat and statesman, including Secretary of State.

Ismael Testé, in the first volume of his work *Ecclesiastical History of Cuba,* writes that Broderick was esteemed by the members of the U.S. government who oversaw negotiating the Cuban church property question, played golf with them often, and, "because of his extremely sympathetic and intelligent character, obtained most of the benefits enjoyed by the Church in Cuba." Likewise, that "he dressed the American, preserving the customs of his country and that he was a young and cheerful man, but of very priestly life." Father Testé wrote that in speaking with the priests that knew him well all agreed that Bishop Broderick was an excellent bishop and that the only things that could have caused the storm against him were his sympathy, joviality, and American customs.[137]

Soon Broderick's affiliations, his popularity among the Cubans, and the success of his brother made him a target for resentment and the rumors that eventually reached Archbishop Chapelle.

Years later, Bishop Broderick would recall, "Mgr. Chapelle was very friendly for a few months, but through the machinations of a member of his family, changed his attitude and began to persecute me atrociously."[138] Who was the family member? It may have been Chapelle's nephew, Father Joseph Solignac, who was serving as secretary to Chapelle in his position as apostolic delegate to Cuba and Puerto Rico. Immediately after Chapelle's death in 1905 Father Solignac went to New Orleans where he "was busy looking over the archbishop's private papers" and "many of the official documents bearing on the archbishop's work in Cuba and Puerto Rico."[139]

One item related to Chapelle that Solignac did not find in his late uncle's papers was a duplicate copy of a receipt dated July 9, 1902. The document acknowledged that Coudert Brothers had received from Broderick a $175,000 bank "draft on Muller, Schall & Co. by H. Upmann & Co., Havana for collection and deposit in Trust Co." The attached letter, dated July 11, stated "It is our present intention to leave $100,000 of this money, when collected, on deposit with the New York Security & Trust company, and deposit the balance, namely $75,000, in the New York Life Insurance Company, 52 Wall Street. These deposits will be made to the joint order of P.L. Chapelle, Apostolic Delegate to Cuba and Porto Rico, and Francisco de Paulo Bernarda, Apostolic Administrator of the Diocese of Havana, or their successors in office." These two items are the only financial documents Broderick kept in his correspondence scrapbook.[140] There is no known explanation why.

The Autumn of his Episcopacy

In the autumn of 1904, Chapelle went to Rome to complain about Broderick, perhaps at the urging of Solignac or of an American named William F. Redding, a long-time resident of Cuba, and no relation to Father William Redding of Unionville who we met in Chapter Three.

William F. Redding's story is seldom told because little is known, but it is a curious one. About 1850, as an orphan eight years of age, he came to America from Ireland. Two years later New York's Archbishop John Hughes took the ten-year-old lad to Cuba on a diocesan visit, where he remained, perhaps adopted. Redding must have been industrious and blessed with excellent social skills and intellect because by the turn of the century he became one of the wealthiest men in Cuba, known and respected by the Vatican. We will meet Mr. Redding again in Chapter Eight.

International Intrigue

Whether at the urging of Redding or Solignac or on his own initiative, Chapelle lodged the complaint that Bishop Broderick had directed lucrative contracts to his brother,[141] adding the damning charge that he had conspired with Juan Antonio Frias, the Cuban politician, to divert funds from the sale of church property on Havana's harbor.[142] It was this latter allegation that would gain traction and become the basis of a 1912 defamation lawsuit brought by Broderick against a magazine, as we will see in Chapter Eight.

Only days behind Chapelle, Broderick arrived in Rome in the fall of 1904, "to protest to the Holy Father against Mgr. Chapelle's persecution of me" and "to request the Holy See send an Apostolic Visitor to Havana to correct the scandalous abuse that prevailed there in the administration of the great number of Pious Foundations that were in existence there."[143]

He took along his mother, and her caretaker-companion, Helen Bowlen. He saw the trip as an opportunity for them to enjoy Rome, perhaps the final time for his seventy-five-year-old mother.

Because he arrived at the Vatican on the heels of Chapelle's visit, rumors that he was in Rome to be appointed apostolic delegate to the Philippines, Chapelle's old post, found their way into the press, a press unaware of the serious allegations Chapelle had brought against him. The Eau Claire, Wisconsin, *Leader-Telegram* even reported that Broderick was thought to be the next bishop of the newly formed Diocese of Superior, Wisconsin.[144]

His time in Rome was not dominated by official meetings. On December 8 he was present in the procession for the closing of the Marian Congress, a session during which he had the opportunity to hear archaeologist Monsignor Joseph Wilpert's talk on his discovery in the Catacomb of Priscilla.[145] On December 16 he celebrated a High Mass in that same catacomb with an added novelty—lighting. "The illumination of the catacomb was an innovation; incandescent electric lamps having been installed." [146] He also made time to visit his earlier archaeological haunts and gather more information for the books he would publish decades later. And in an audience with Pius X, he presented his mother to the pope, together with Phoebe Hearst, mother of William Randolph Hearst,[147] who, at the time, was a member of Congress representing part of Manhattan. Mrs. Hearst may have been celebrating her birthday in Europe; she had turned 63 on December 3.

The main event of course was his response to the claims made by Chapelle. He offered his defense and explanation to Pius X and Cardinal Merry del Val, the Cardinal Secretary of State. Sympathetic to his predicament, the pope resolved that rather than return to Havana, Broderick should resign his Cuban episcopacy and return to the U.S. with a new assignment. The pope created a novel position, with national responsibilities, to accommodate Broderick's proven skill in financial matters. Though his resignation as Auxiliary Bishop of Havana would not be official for several months the future course was decided on December 17 while he was still in Rome. His resignation, to be effective May 1, was made public and announced on January

9 by Havana's *El Diario de la Marina*. In a document dated December 17, written in Italian, and signed by Merry del Val, he was given a *pensio* of $100 per month.

The pope determined that Broderick should return to U.S. in an administrative position, live in Washington, and work "in the religious interests of the Church."[148] It was understood and publicized that his work would include the organization and promotion of the Peter's Pence collection in each diocese in the United States, while serving as auxiliary bishop to Cardinal Gibbons of Baltimore.

Broderick accepted but was unhappy with the outcome and felt that Merry del Val "was deadly hostile" to him and that his new position was, in his words, one "for which, it appeared, I had talent but no liking."[149] He must have felt a tinge of *déjà vu*, reminiscent of 1900 when Bishop Tierney wanted him to leave Hartford though he insisted he had done nothing wrong.

Peter's Pence, a donation to the Successor of Peter, took on stable form in the seventh century, first with the conversion of the Anglo-Saxons and in the following centuries across Europe as more citizens adhered to Christianity. It is an offering that supports the needs of the entire Church, especially in those places where the Church experiences greater difficulties.[150] The need for an increased focus on the collection was fueled by troubles between the Church and the French government resulting in a decrease in the Vatican's French income.

Broderick was advised by both the Holy Father and Archbishop Pietro Gasparri, then Secretary for the Commission for the Codification of Canon Law, to remain in Rome for a period but he, his mother, and Helen Bowlen returned to America, crossing the Atlantic on the *S.S. Ivernia*, a Cunard Lines ship, leaving Liverpool on January 18 and arriving in Boston on January 27.[151]

In time he would be asked to explain why he left Rome against the suggestion of the pope and Gasparri.[152] "I thought it would be worse than useless for me to remain because (Merry del Val) would probably use his great power to make my life there miserable and useless," and "out of the immediately preceding fourteen years, I had spent twelve away from the United States, and, in consequence, felt a great nostalgia for my own country."[153]

Broderick may not have been thrilled with his new assignment, but the Catholic press in America was, as reported in the February 14 issue of *The Catholic Union and Times* of Buffalo, New York:

> Monsignor B. F. Broderick, formerly of Hartford, Conn., but more recently known through his masterful efforts to get order out of the chaos of Cuban ecclesiastical finances, spent three or four days (in Washington) last week. He was enroute to Havana from Rome, where he was cordially received by the Holy Father, the Papal Secretary of State, Cardinal Merry del Val and the officials of the Propaganda Fide. Mgr. Broderick will spend but a short time in Havana and will then return to Washington to establish the national American headquarters for the collection of the Peter's Pence. He was entrusted with this important mission by Cardinal Merry del Val by reason of his eminent qualifications. He was successful in establishing a solid financial basis for the Church in Havana. even beyond the hopes of his friends. He accomplished also that difficult task of gain-

ing the esteem of government officials as well as the confidences of the people.[154]

He made a brief visit to Cuba, which provided a third reason for his leaving Rome against the suggestion of the pope and Gasparri. "I was anxious to go back to Havana and settle my business affairs there, as I was penniless except for the several thousands of dollars that were owed to me by the Diocese of Havana. I wished to collect that and to use it for establishing my mother —who was then 75 years old—in a home where she would be comfortable ... "[155]

He left Havana on February 28,[156] with a letter of the same date penned in Spanish by Cuba's President Estrada Palma, addressing him as "My distinguished and respected friend." Palma acknowledged the zeal displayed by Broderick in performance of his "high mission as Coadjutor Bishop of the Diocese of Havana" and recognizing his "sympathy for the people of Cuba."[157]

Within days of his return, the *Philadelphia Inquirer* carried a report that hinted at growing discontent among the American hierarchy over his new assignment. Datelined New York, March 4, the brief article read:

> Right Rev. B. Broderick, Auxiliary Bishop of Havana, who has been entrusted with a mission to this country by Pope Pius X, arrived here today from Havana. He will leave at once for Washington. Bishop Broderick's mission is of a confidential nature and has to do with urging greater offerings of Peter's Pence in the United States because of the relations existing between France and the Holy See. Recent dispatches from Rome indicate that more or less dissatisfaction exists in this country as a result of Bishop Broderick's mission.[158]

The Crash

American bishops were dumbfounded and wanted nothing to do with a central administration of the annual collection. An uprising among the episcopacy quickly ensued, fueled by a mid-February visit to New Orleans by Gibbons that included a two-day meeting with Chapelle.[159] Within weeks of the Chapelle-Gibbons conference the entire plan of Pius X for Bishop Broderick collapsed with a mighty thud.

The *New York Times* described the rebellion under the headline "The Vatican Yields to American Bishops."

> Owing to complaints which have been received (in Rome), the Vatican has withdrawn from Mgr. Broderick, Auxiliary Bishop of Havana, the mission entrusted to him to urge American Bishops to increase the collection of Peter's Pence.
>
> There has been little public discussion about the matter since the announcement of the appointment of Msgr. Broderick was made. Privately, however, the bishops all over the country were known to be opposed to the move. How far they went toward making their displeasure felt is not generally known."[160]

The private opposition soon became public. The bishops gathered in Washington where the city's *Evening Star* reported, "It is understood that the archbishops prefer the old method rather than the innovation proposed with (Bishop) Broderick as the officer in charge of the fund. It is said that if the archbishops are reluctant to transmit their funds through (Bishop) Broderick's hands instead of directly to the pope, the formation of the proposed new office will be abandoned."[161] Cardinal Gibbons, in "unaccustomed firmness"[162] had vetoed the Peter's Pence assignment.

Gibbons harbored a suspicion that the assignment might have been Broderick's idea, and not that of Pius X. A New York City lawyer investigated the matter, reporting his findings to Gibbons. That lawyer was Amasa Thornton, who had connections to the Vatican dating back to Leo XIII. Thornton was not a stranger to controversy and his association with Gibbons in the matter is a curious one as the lawyer and Chapelle had a fractured and publicly contentious relationship dating back to 1899.

On March 10 Thornton wrote to Gibbons: "I had a long interview with Bishop Broderick yesterday afternoon and this morning. I am satisfied that the idea of having him collect Peter's Pence was the Holy Father's," adding,

> I am satisfied the Holy Father intended that he should keep his relations with the Diocese of Havana, because he has ordered the Bishop of Havana to pay him one hundred dollars a month until further notice. Knowing what I know of the situation in Cuba, Your Eminence, I believe that Bishop Broderick should be sent back there at once to look after the Church property and do nothing else, keeping out of the religious and spiritual work of the church entirely. I have written Archbishop Ireland to the same effect, and I think for the sake of the Church property steps should be taken immediately to have him sent back to Cuba, as evidently the Holy Father expected he might be.[163]

As late as March 29, the pope, after acquiescing to the pressure brought to bear over the Peter's Pence debacle, was still considering Broderick's future. In a handwritten letter to Broderick, the pope explained to him that, yes, he had withdrawn the Peter's Pence assignment, but also that "it was not an easy thing for him to provide a diocese *immediately* to Bishop Broderick. The Holy Father referred to Bishop Broderick's plight as a small trial, indicating that at least up to that time there had been no grave charges against the bishop."[164]

But Gibbons wanted to torpedo both parts of the Vatican's plan for Broderick, the Peter's Pence assignment and the appointment as his auxiliary bishop. Having succeeded with the former, he pursued the latter, writing to Merry del Val on March 31, 1905:[165]

> A few days ago, His Excellency, (Archbishop Diomede Falconio) the Apostolic Delegate[166] approached me on the subject of allowing Mgr. Broderick the privilege of exercising in Washington certain episcopal functions. Fearful of the consequences of such action on the part of the Monsignor, I feel it is my duty to again appeal to your Eminence. I do not see of what possible service he could be to me in Washington. The Catholic population of that city does not exceed 40,000 and the presence of myself and my auxiliary is sufficient.

He continued, introducing other concerns:

> Not one of the pastors in the city of Washington would ever invite Msgr. Broderick to confirm because for some years minds have been turned against him.
> In addition to this, to be candid, I must admit that on account of certain rumors rife in that city, Washington would be the last place in the world for Mgr. Broderick's residence. I do not inquire into the merits of these reports, nor do I pronounce upon them. I only know that

they came to Washington as it is the seat of government and further believe it is highly possible that documents of a similar nature may be found in some of the departments.

And, in a most damning assessment, he wrote "In light of this fact, I think the position and residence in Washington would be most trying to Mgr. Broderick, and in the end would result in the mortification of Catholics in America."

Gibbons does his best to conclude charitably, with a recommendation gleaned from Thornton's letter: "I am certainly of the opinion that it would be well to regulate Mgr. Broderick's affairs as soon as possible in a prudent manner, and as he is very conversant with the Spanish language, he may yet be able to do some good in Cuba, or thereabouts, or even in the Philippines."

Snubbed by Gibbons, Broderick sought Rome's intervention with an ill-timed written plea for an assignment. Sadly, his letter ended up causing what turned out to be a grave self-inflicted wound. Whether an error in translation or poor communication between the pope and his staff, the letter was misunderstood in Rome. Broderick simply wanted the pope to understand that a bishop idled in America without a diocese would appear scandalous to some, but Pius X interpreted his concern otherwise. In a handwritten letter the pope replied, "I do not hide from you the heavy sorrow that you have brought to my heart, by your threat, in your letter, to cause a grave scandal."[167]

That was the last Broderick heard from the Holy Father. No one knows why Pius X offered no further communication on the matter during the remaining ten years of his pontificate but judging by the immediate action Broderick took he knew his separation from the Church would not soon change.

Did Broderick appeal to the Apostolic Delegate, or others? No evidence has surfaced that he did. Perhaps he was convinced that two of the most powerful men on both sides of the Atlantic, Gibbons in America and Merry del Val in Rome, were so intent on ostracizing him that he felt he had no recourse.

The Titular Bishop of Juliopolis was now set adrift; his only consolation, if there be one, was his $100 *pensio* that placed him among the top two percent of all wage-earners in the United States.[168] It was a time when a pair of shoes cost two dollars, a topcoat five, a pound of apples twelve cents, a sirloin steak twenty cents, and a six-room apartment in Manhattan could be rented for five dollars a week.[169]

It was a moment of confusion. Still in good standing with the Church, but with severed ties, he faced an uncertain future. True to form, the ambitious young man of thirty-six was not idled long. Though he remained true to his priestly vows, he immediately took on a new mission in the secular world. In his usual restless fashion, he made his way into the White House for a private meeting with President Roosevelt to present his plan and solicit the support of the president.

6. Early Years of Exile, 1905–1911

Following his February visit to Havana,[170] Broderick moved into the New Amsterdam Hotel at the corner of 4th Avenue (now Park Avenue South) and 21st Street in Manhattan,[171] while his mother and Helen Bowlen resided at 2 Tower Place in Yonkers, the residence purchased a few years earlier.

The Move to Staatsburg

In August, the family moved north to Staatsburg, as reported in the *Poughkeepsie Semi-Weekly Eagle:* "A new resident of Dutchess County is Bishop Broderick, formerly Roman Catholic bishop of Cuba (who) purchased the beautiful Parker place at Staatsburg, the first place north of Dinsmore's. He is now a titular bishop, having retired from active work, and lives in his new home with his mother. Bishop Broderick is one of the most cultured men in the church of this country."[172]

Dinsmore's was one of the famous Staatsburg mansions of the Gilded Age, a four-story, 92-room Italianate-style mansion nestled among 1,000 acres.[173] The Dinsmores had a private nine-hole golf course, which would have been an attraction for Broderick, who enjoyed the nascent sport.

How could Broderick afford such an estate? He had his *pensio* and the "several thousands of dollars" owed him by the Diocese of Havana but it was his friend from Branford, Margaret Plant Graves, the multimillionaire widow of Henry B. Plant who aided the acquisition of the Parker place. Mary M. Parker sold the property to Margaret Graves in 1905.[174]

For the next thirty years Broderick, and his mother until her death, and Helen Bowlen, straddled both sides of the Hudson River; New York, Westchester, and Dutchess counties to the east; Ulster County to the west; and for a few summers, the bishop would live in Vermont.

Renaissance Man

Resigned to earning a living outside the Church, he sought a line of work pastoral in nature and in keeping with his life experience. Resourceful and inventive, he turned his focus to the issue of settling immigrants, with a particular plan for those coming to America from Italy whose point of arrival was New York.

He told reporters that although this plan had occupied his attention for several years, it was only on a recent trip to Washington on papal business that conditions there persuaded him that the time was ripe for putting it into effect.[175]

The genesis of the invitation is not known, but on May 24, just weeks into his separation, he appeared at a meeting of The Southern Industrial Parliament in Washington, D.C. where he delivered an address titled "Italian Settlement in the Southern States." His speech was accompanied by a booklet with the complete text of his address; an original is found in the Collection Department of Widener Library at Harvard University.[176]

There is a remarkable handwritten note in the booklet found at Harvard: "Koiner said he couldn't understand why Catholic priests were taking so much interest in this movement. Catholics formed about 3% of our foundation."

The "Koiner" the unknown note writer refers to was George W. Koiner, the Virginia State Commissioner of Agriculture, who, according to Baltimore's *Sun*, was "making unusual efforts to attract a good class of immigrants to Virginia. Mr. Koiner says he does not want any refuse element, but desires the intelligent, thrifty class, from Great Britain, Germany and other countries, men who have a knowledge of farming, and desire to better their condition."[177]

One reason Catholic priests were taking an interest was the respect many priests held for Pope Leo XIII's 1891 encyclical on capital and labor, *Rerum Novarum*. The document, today considered to have birthed modern Catholic social teaching, took to task the new economic order resulting from the global growth of industry, bringing to the fore new concerns for the dignity of work and the rights of workers.

As for Broderick's personal interest, his answer is found in the speech itself: "It is indeed a source of great pleasure to me to set forth before this distinguished assemblage of representative businessmen of the great New South my views on one of the most vital questions of the political and industrial well-being of our glorious nation." After outlining the history of immigration and the debate surrounding immigrant regulation, he said "I believe in the distribution of immigrants instead of the restriction of immigration."

Why his emphasis on connecting Italian immigrants with agriculture? He explained: "I selected the Italians because they represent nearly forty percent of the entire immigration at the present time, because they are the most practical agricultural people on the face of the earth today, and because seven years spent among them has given me a complete knowledge of their manners, customs, language, etc."

Following the speech, *The Washington Post* editorialized support for Broderick in the strongest terms: "There is probably no man in this country who knows Italy and the Italian people more thoroughly than the learned and philanthropic Bishop Broderick of Havana, who is now in Washington." The editorial continued,

> This knowledge was not gained by reading, but by actual contact with the people of Italy during his eight years' residence in Rome. In that time, he traveled over every part of the kingdom, mastered the language, and familiarized himself with Italian customs and institutions "Here is a country," said Bishop Broderick in conversation at the Raleigh, "that has about the area of the State of Georgia so far as arable land is concerned, and yet it supports a population of 36,000,000, nearly all of whom get their living from the soil. Here is a race of people industrious, frugal, and law abiding. In my opinion it would be a fine thing for the Southern States of America to get a large Italian influx, and this, indeed, may prove a solution of the labor problem for the South."[178]

Broderick's plan of "distributing Italian immigrants" was brought to the attention of Booker T. Washington, the influential spokesman for Black Americans. In a letter[179] from a Mr. W. B. Watkins of Richmond, Virginia, the writer connects Broderick to Terence Powderly,[180] a well-known labor union leader and long-serving immigration official:

> At a so-called Immigration Convention in Washington ... one Bonaventure F. Broderick, a Roman Catholic

Bishop delivered an address strongly advocating Italians for the South. The fact that Powderly[181] is a Catholic is another reason why he is trying to force Italians on the South.

The Italian American Agricultural Association

Gaining traction, he soon took his plan to the next level. On November 9, accompanied by Adolfo Rossi, the Italian foreign ministry's travelling emigration inspector, he met with President Theodore Roosevelt in the White House to present his plan.[182] Broderick had little trouble securing a meeting with Roosevelt. If needed, letters of introduction were readily available to him from Elihu Root, or more likely, General Leonard Wood. The bishop's relationship with Wood was solidified in Cuba through Church property negotiations and on the golf course, while Roosevelt found the adventuresome Wood, a one-time fellow Rough Rider, to represent "everything he admired in an American male."[183]

Within weeks of the November meeting and with the support of the president, the Italian American Agricultural Association (IAAA) was incorporated with Broderick as president and treasurer.

The IAAA was approved by Frank Sargent, the Commissioner General of Immigration who spoke highly of the program to *The Washington Post*:

> The establishment of this bureau meets with my heartiest approval. If such bureaus were extended so as to take in immigrants from all countries it would be of inestimable benefit to this country. The great thing we have always had to contend with is the congestion of

> people in the large cities. Especially is this noticeable in New York where people of every nation on earth have their own particular little colony to which immigrants flock according to their nativity. There they hear familiar tongues, get home foods, enjoy native customs and thus cause congestion. After these people have settled among their own race it is almost impossible to induce them to venture elsewhere.[184]

And in the south, the *Tampa Tribune* of February 7, 1906, carried a front-page announcement, headlined "Italians for the South."

> Supported by ample capital and many of the foremost philanthropists of the country, among them President Roosevelt, the Italian American Agriculture Association has been incorporated, for the purpose of colonizing Italian immigrants in the South. Bishop Bonaventure F. Broderick. Titular Bishop of Juliopolis, who has spent many years in Italy, Spain, Cuba and other Latin countries, is president and treasurer of the association, and has associated with him a group of men of wealth and business prominence in various parts of the country."[185]

The central part of the plan was to secure large tracts of land and settle colonies of Italians, with their families and all necessary community amenities, including churches, schools, and stores. Each such tract would provide acreage for farming with the association also supplying the buildings; the fully equipped farms turned over to Italian families at cost.

A colony was planned in Waycross, Georgia negotiated by Broderick with George W. Deen, a Georgia state senator, banker, and regional land developer, as reported by the *Atlanta Constitution* on March 23, 1906:[186]

> George W. Deen is making arrangements for the establishment of an Italian colony in this county. The Colony will be located on Mr. Deen's land between this city and Astoria and about three miles from Waycross.
>
> For some time, Mr. Deen has been in correspondence with Rev. Bonaventure F. Broderick of Staatsburg, New York, a Catholic bishop regarding the establishment of a colony here. Rev. Broderick is an Italian and has brought many of his people from Italy to America and established colonies for them.
>
> He has made an agreement with Mr. Deen to furnish twenty-five Italian families for Ware County. Mr. Deen will use them for work in a sawmill which he will erect south of Waycross. He proposes to furnish the Italians with from 20 to 40 acres of farmland and construct for each family a home of at least three rooms. While the men are employed at the sawmill the women and children will clear and cultivate the farm.
>
> The Italians will be brought direct to this country from Italy and will be furnished an interpreter until they are acquainted with the language here. Bishop Broderick agrees to send to Ware County only industrious Italian families and assures Mr. Deen that they will make good citizens.

His plan was hailed in 1906 in "The Village, A Journal of Village Life," the article proclaiming, "Bishop Broderick's plan of village planting for the attraction of Italians is so compact, so suggestive, that it is outlined here for the encouragement of Italian village building, in the South and Southwest particularly."

The diagram that accompanied the article illustrated Broderick's plan for each colony beginning with one square mile, 640 acres, and thirty-two farms of twenty acres each.

The piece concluded confidently: "It is practically certain from demonstrations that have been made over and over again in this country that the settlement of a small number in this way once secured, will need no further artificial stimulus. The little settlements will expand as surely and naturally as the growth of a banyan tree." The optimism had a bias to it: the author was Eliot Lord, who was not only a journalist, but was a director of the IAAA and author of the book *The Italian in America*, published in 1906 by B. F. Buck, also an officer of the IAAA.

The Sin of Peonage

At the time there were many similar societies and associations, often organized with an ethnic focus, aiming to help immigrants acclimate to the country. Most were efficient at supplying social and other accommodations but were less effective at securing employment for their members. This opened the door for labor employment agencies. Most were honorable, but some lacked integrity. Many unsuspecting immigrants fell victim to unsavory labor agents and labor practices. Peonage, the forced human slavery through debt, was a nascent problem. Broderick, through no fault of his own, did not escape this albatross.

From the onset he tackled his duties with his customary zeal and energy, predicting the "Go West" slogan of Horace Greely would soon be replaced by "Go South, young man,"[187] but confidence aside, his affiliation with the association was to be short-lived, due to yet another controversy beyond his control. By the summer of 1906, his name was in the press again, this time the result of the indictment and arraignment of Mr. Sigmund S. Schwartz, the owner of a New York labor employment agency.

The case began with the July arrest of Schwartz, charged with peonage, based on the complaint of Bennie Wilenski. "Wilenski stated in his affidavit that Schwartz had made such fine representation to him that he had gone down to Florida where he had been horribly maltreated and forced to work in the swamps until he succeeded in making his escape."[188]

Schwartz protested that he knew nothing of the alleged treatment of men he sent south, and that he sent them to the Hodges, O'Hara and Russell Co. in Florida at the request of Francis de Lauzieres, "a French Swiss Sunday School teacher in the Italian Episcopal Church of San Salvatore on Elizabeth Street," who he claimed was from an organization called the Southern Agricultural Colonization Society.[189] Mr. de Lauzieres testified that he knew nothing about the Florida lumber company except that he had been told by Mr. B. F. Buck, the third-vice-president of the Italian American Agriculture Association to get as many laborers as he could for the Hodges company. *The Sun* of New York picks up the story from here:

> M. de Lauzieres then went to Schwartz and told him that Bishop Bonaventure F. Broderick formerly of Havana was interested in getting Italian colonists settled in the South. Schwartz said that it would be difficult to get Italians with families, but he could get good men, the agreement being that the Italian American Agricultural Society should pay him $2 a head for each man sent down. De Lauzieres told Schwartz that the lumber company would like to get men who would be willing to buy ten- or twenty-acre sections of land at $3 to $5 an acre

and was willing to give the men seven years to pay for the land, provided they would work for the company.

Schwartz then suggested that no mention of the land be made as it might be difficult to get men to go South if they thought they were to get no money for their work. De Lauzieres was emphatic in his assertions that Bishop Broderick knew nothing about alleged peonage camps. He said that the Bishop, who now is at Stattsburgh, was the treasurer of the Italian American Agricultural Society and as such paid Schwartz for the men sent South.[190]

The case against Schwartz got its start when Wilenski's treatment came to the attention of a thirty-five-year-old lawyer named Mary Grace Quackenbos, who would become famously nicknamed "Mrs. Sherlock Holmes" for her investigative prowess. Her tenacity in following up on Wilenski's story led to a federal investigation of Florida lumber, turpentine, and railroad camps. Schwartz, and other labor employment agents were found guilty.[191] Broderick was never accused of complicity or having knowledge of any mistreatment, thus confirming the testimony of Francis de Lauzieres.

Cuba Reconsidered

Annoyed over yet another uninvited controversy complicating his life, he soon distanced himself from the IAAA, redirecting his energy to a new enterprise again involving people and geography he was familiar with: Cuba and business and industry acquaintances from his time on the island.

He was approached by Hugh J. Reilly, Sr., the Boston contractor he met in Havana six years earlier. Reilly was engaged in the construction of aqueducts and sewage systems in the city of Cienfuegos on Cuba's south-central coast, and he asked Broderick to find laborers for the project. Broderick went to Cuba, a three-day voyage from New York, to investigate the project, returning on the *S.S. Morro Castle,* arriving at Ellis Island on June 20, 1906.

A few months later he made a second trip: "Bishop Bonaventure Broderick is spending some time in Cuba looking over some interests that he has located there," the *Poughkeepsie Eagle*[192] reported on November 6 in a column simply titled "Dutchess County" that chronicled newsworthy events of residents.

Not only local papers, but his renewed interest in the island also caught the attention of the editorializing city papers. New York's *The Sun*, in reporting on a story involving politician Juan Antonio Frias and his use of former cemetery property included a sideways glance at Havana's former auxiliary bishop: "The Espada was one of the oldest cemeteries in Cuba. Through the influence of Bishop Broderick who has left Cuba, not altogether, say his enemies, to the detriment of the island, Frias came into possession of this ancient city of the dead. It was his purpose to employ the land for commercial purposes."[193]

After Broderick's second trip, Reilly's sewage system project stalled when a new wave of civil unrest on the island brought construction to a halt and the need for immigrant labor was diminished, idling the bishop for a brief period, during which time he continued to seek secular business opportunities, networking in New York and Washington.

After American troops were sent to Cuba and the civil unrest subdued, Broderick made two more trips to Havana on behalf of Reilly's project. The first is marked by his arrival home at Ellis Island on the swift *Saratoga* on July 11, 1907, and the second when he returned on the *S.S. Marida* on October 29. Finally, in 1908 the rebellion was quelled, and work restarted on the project. The same year he turned his palatial Staatsburg home over to Margaret Plant Graves[194] and moved back to Yonkers with his mother and Helen Bowlen to 15 Tower Place, near their earlier residence at 2 Tower Place.[195]

The Donovan & Phillips Company

As general contractor, Reilly engaged several subcontractors on the Cienfuegos sewer project, a contract valued at nearly $4 million. The list included the Donovan & Philipps Co., owned by Simon Donovan, an experienced builder of sewer systems, and George Phillips, the former Superintendent of Sewers in Boston. In the next chapter we will read the details of how Messrs. Donovan and Phillips came to distrust each other and finally abandoned the project in 1909; their breakup opened the door for Broderick and John A Sullivan to take ownership of the company.

In the legal drama unfolding in the next chapter, we will read the details of how, beginning in 1909 and continuing through 1912, Broderick administered the domestic affairs of Donovan & Phillips Co. from New York, and how his brother, David, was hired to oversee the construction site in Cuba, assisted by Hugh "Hughey" Reilly, Jr., son of the general contractor. Little did any of them know, at the outset, how the prosperous venture would stress their relationships and lead to litigation.[196]

It is interesting to note that the same year, Hamersly's *Who's Who in New York and State*[197] made no mention of his ownership of Donovan & Phillips Co., but rather records his position as "General Commissioner of the Pope for the Collection of the

Peter's Pence." As this information was likely submitted to the editor by Broderick, it is telling that, for some reason, he was still holding on to that title.

Inheritance of an Old Friend

The year 1909 brought another curious development to the bishop's story when, on May 30, Margaret Plant Graves passed away at age eighty, but the intrigue began with her first husband's death ten years earlier in 1899.[198] Though Henry B. Plant's estate was valued at more than $20 million, he left Margaret, his second wife, only a solitary pension of $30,000 a year. The vast bulk of his estate was left to his grandson's unborn children. The grandson was eight years old at the time![199]

Whether it was Henry's intention to create a family quarrel over his last will and testament is not known, but one ensued, involving Margaret and Morton Plant, Henry's adult son from his first marriage, and his only child. One item of contention was the famous Tampa Bay Hotel, the resort hotel built by Plant in 1891 that stands today. Margaret wanted to pass the entire property to the Society of Jesus, the religious order of priests and brothers known as the Jesuits. In the end, she reluctantly gave it over to Morton.[200] It took several years of legal bickering in courtrooms in Connecticut and New York, but in January of 1904, five years after Henry's death, Margaret received a settlement estimated to be $7 million.

Five months after receiving the settlement, and already a rich widow, she became even wealthier when she wed Robert Graves, Jr., a millionaire inventor of electrical devices who had inherited a fortune from his father, whose treasure was earned over several decades through his Bronx wallpaper business, the Robert

Graves Company. When she died, her estate was valued at $8 million.

Margaret, unlike Chappelle and Gibbons, had confidence in Broderick's handling of finances: she left him $25,000 and named him co-executor with lawyer Frederick J. Middlebrook of New York "without bond."[201] Requiring a bond would have placed a greater measure of accountability on the executors; its absence shows Margaret Graves had a great deal of trust in the two men. She knew Middlebrook through her first husband; Middlebrook was an heir to the Bradish Johnson estate. Johnson, a wealthy industrialist who owned sugar plantations and refineries in Louisiana, died in 1892.[202]

In addition to his $25,000 inheritance, and his $100 monthly *pensio*, Broderick was earning a healthy income managing the domestic affairs of the Cienfuegos project. He began to accumulate rental property in the Bronx and elsewhere in the New York area. In 1910, he, his mother and Helen Bowlen spent several months in Europe before returning on the *S.S. Megantic*, sailing from Liverpool to Quebec and crossing the border at St. Albans, Vermont on October 14.

Villa Marguerite in Saugerties

After their return from Europe the bishop bought an estate of 200 acres, located in the Barclay Heights neighborhood of Saugerties, Ulster County, on the west side of the Hudson, more than 100 miles north of Yonkers. He bought the property from Louis Washburn of the Washburn brickmaking family and renamed it Villa Marguerite in honor of his mother.

The substantial purchase captured the attention of the neighboring public, and the *Kingston Daily Freeman* reported that the new owner was updating and modernizing the house. True to form, Broderick did not shun publicity. When asked by the journalist why he bought the country home, he replied, "I thought I would turn from parasite to producer. I would live where I could raise most of what we eat. As an English king remarked, 'I would live mostly of my own.' I came here for country life where I may live close to nature, read and study. But more than all to give my mother a home. She is past eighty and the climate agrees with her."[203]

The reporter's visit took place in April of 1912. He describes Villa Marguerite as "the home of Bishop B. F. Broderick, in the diplomatic service of the Church of Rome at Washington," implying again that he continued to await instructions from Rome. At some level, emotionally or otherwise, he was holding on to the ill-fated Peter's Pence assignment of 1905.

The reporter, identified as Mr. Fox, describes the impressive setting: "We entered broad grounds, the drives shaded with tall, shapely locusts and oaks. Widely open to commanding views, this squarely built residence with thick, gray concreted walls and deep window casements in manse style, plate glass and ornamental gables, rises into view from considerable distances. A country home, it is as equipped as the latest improved city home; electric lights and gas fittings; improved toilets and baths and sanitary plumbing."

Mr. Fox continued his tour inside: "From its broad porch glimpses are caught of the waters of the Hudson. The beautiful carvings, tiled floor, and highly finished casements of the vestibule with massive doors of beveled glass ushered us into large rooms finished in natural wood, delicately tinted walls, genteel furnishings, richly built stairs and polished newels, chandeliers, rugs, and art souvenirs."

The considerable estate, with its emphasis on agriculture, required several employees and the local papers seemed anxious to keep track of the comings and goings of the staff, including chauffeurs,[204] and even tidbits such as: "Bishop Broderick of Barclay Heights has engaged Kenneth Bogardus to clean his entire house with Mr. Bogardus's liquid cleaning process."[205] And in 1913 it was reported "Bishop Broderick has a large patch of peanuts growing on his property on Barclay Heights, near Saugerties. They are of the Burpee variety."[206]

Soon Broderick was known throughout Ulster County and was in demand as a speaker. One early invitation came from Poultney Bigelow:

> At the invitation of Poultney Bigelow, the distinguished Prima Donna, Inez Barbour,[207] has consented to come from New York and sing at the inauguration of the Malden-on-Hudson Recreation Hall on November 13, Sunday afternoon. The Rt. Rev. B. F. Broderick, the new Catholic bishop, will make the address. The proceeds are to be devoted to public improvements of a nonsectarian character.[208]

Bigelow, journalist, author of eleven books, and global traveler, is another link in Broderick's vast networking. A graduate of Yale, and Columbia Law School, he was the son of John Bigelow, Abraham Lincoln's ambassador to France.[209] The following year he donated a new library to his hometown in Malden-on-the-Hudson and Broderick was again invited to speak at the dedication.

He had hoped to spend his time at Villa Marguerite reading and studying, but ill winds of discontent were blowing through the offices of lawyers in New York and Boston, some driven by the decade-old accusations of Chapelle, Gibbons and company and others by the riches gained from the Cienfuegos sewer system contract. Before these ill winds reached Saugerties and the tranquility of Villa Marguerite, another uninvited controversy took root in an unexpected place.

7. More Turmoil: Gossip and Legal Drama, 1912–1915

During the summer of 1911, while Broderick was engaged in managing the domestic affairs of the Donovan & Phillips Co., salacious gossip began to circulate. Where it had its genesis is unknown, but it gained traction in a most unlikely setting: the dining hall of St. Agnes Convent in Baltimore.

One day that summer, an otherwise pleasant table conversation among visiting ladies and religious sisters was derailed by the assertion of one of the visitors that Bishop Broderick was a married man. The alleged spouse? His mother's companion and caretaker, Helen Bowlen, who had been living in the Broderick home ten years. The gossip reached New York's archbishop, Cardinal John Farley, who did not sit idly by.

The Diary Labeled "The Case of Bishop Broderick is Recited in the Following Pages"

Inside a small red leather-bound 1912 diary, blank until the page for February 10 where, written in script, are the words, "The Case of Bishop Broderick is recited in the following pages."[210]

On the page for February 11 is written, "Mgr. Cerretti today made the following statement in re: Broderick. He says he was informed of the marriage of Broderick to the person who has been living with him for years." Cerretti at the time was an auditor affiliated with the Apostolic Delegation in Washington.

Seemingly unbeknownst to Broderick at the time (and no evidence has surfaced that he ever became aware of the inquiry) the investigation into his marital status was undertaken by Farley assisted by Father Kenny, the pastor of St. Mary's in Saugerties, where Broderick was living at Villa Marguerite.

Included with the diary are letters clarifying the gossip. A woman named "Miss Rourke," and another named "Miss Drain" were the key players. Drain was the informant who told the tale to Cerretti after hearing it from Rourke, who vocalized the rumor at the lunch table. Rourke was from Savannah, Georgia and was visiting her sister who was a religious Sister of Mercy at the convent in Baltimore.

Cerretti, after speaking with Miss Drain, wrote the following report to Farley:

> Miss Drain told me it was last summer when she heard of the report. She does not remember how the conversation turned to B..., but she does remember very well it was a lady who gave the report in the presence of a few Sisters. That lady, speaking of B... said: That man is the ruin of Religion in the U.S., he has married a woman who has been a Novice and who has lived with him since she left the Convent. The Sisters and Miss Drain were terribly shocked at that statement, and Miss Drain asked the lady: are you sure that B... has married the woman? Yes, I am, answered the lady. Then all those present commented on the scandal which the statement would occasion.[211]

Cardinal Farley then wrote to Miss Rourke in Savannah:

> Dear Madam:
>
> I have been informed by a reliable party that on occasion of a visit to St. Agnes Convent of Mercy, Balt., you stated that you know that M. Broderick was married. I presume you know to whom I refer as being married.
>
> You are also reported to have made the above statement in the presence of more than one person, and that your sister, a Sister of Mercy of that convent was present when you made the remark. It is also said that some of those present on the occasion asked you if you were quite sure and if what you said was true. You answered, "I am quite sure he is married."
>
> Now the gentleman lives in this diocese, and as the truth or falsehood of the rumored marriage is a matter of very great importance as you must understand, I pray you in all charity and most earnestly for the sake of religion be so nice to let us know the source of your information.
>
> I shall regard whatever you may be pleased to communicate in the matter as most confidential.[212]

Miss Rourke responded to Farley on June 14:

> I have received your most gracious favor of the seventh instant and would be pleased to furnish you with information you seek, but it is not in my power to do so. At the outset I desire to correct the impression gained from your informant in New York and who was as I have stated then unnamed. I joined in the conversation and when I became aware that it was the same party, I stated that I had heard he was married. On being questioned relating to his status I replied that I know little or

nothing about him but that I felt sure I had heard in New York that he was married. This information was communicated to me as a rumor and the party who gave it was in no position to prove it, and I so stated at the time. I deeply regret that I have been misquoted to your Eminence in the matter. Your informant has misquoted me when she said I stated I was sure Broderick was married.[213]

There is no indication Farley was hoping to find something amiss but if he were he must have thrown up his hands in despair when he received a report from Father Kenny in Saugerties who wrote that Helen Bowlen, who must have been seen about town with a gentleman, was "according to rumor engaged to be married."[214]

Kenny's report was incredibly detailed, even flattering, the opposite of what Farley may have expected:

> The place he occupies is called Villa Marguerite—comprising about one hundred acres, not on the main road, and bordering on the Esopus Creek.
> The household consists of his mother, quite old and somewhat enfeebled from rheumatism. Miss Helen Boland (sic), companion to his mother and housekeeper —according to rumor engaged to be married. Maud Burso, a parishioner, not long in his employ—a good woman and practical Catholic, a maid servant.
> Dress: Always wears Pectoral Cross and Ring, even when helping on the farm.
> Habits: Celebrates Mass every Sunday and holyday, and perhaps during the week. I could not learn definitely about the weekday Masses. His mother receives Holy Communion at his Masses.

He is charitable and kind, dignified in his manner and bearing.

The people regard him highly and attribute his manner of living to the poor health of himself and his mother—this they think, is the reason for resigning his see.

In the beginning his presence occasioned some comment, but that has passed.

I can state positively that no unfavorable criticism or even the slightest suspicion regarding him has reached me.[215]

A summary of the investigation was prepared by then-Chancellor of the archdiocese, Monsignor Patrick Hayes and sent to Cardinal Merry del Val at the Vatican.[216]

Within months the controversy fizzled and Cerretti wrote to Farley on June 23, 1912: "Whatever it may be, I think that the report is not certain and even were it so it would be impossible to unearth it. In my opinion what originated the report was the fact of the presence of that person in the house of M. B. No wonder if some people who know his career take it for granted that he married that person."[217]

The Mysterious Helen Bowlen

Her birth name was Margaret Helen Bowlen, the daughter of Helen Boyle, a native of New Jersey and Patrick Bowlen, a native of Dublin, Ireland. She received the Sacrament of Confirmation on May 17, 1891, at St. Peter's Church in Quincy Illinois.[218] On October 24, 1897, at the age of nineteen, she entered the novitiate of the Sisters of the Good Shepherd and received the holy habit of religion in the Monastery of Our Lady of Charity of the Good Shepherd in St. Louis, Missouri. At the time her mother was living in Jacksonville, Illinois and her father in Lewiston, Montana.[219]

> The order is one which stands unique in its purpose. Named "the Sisters of the Good Shepherd," the great object of these nuns is to save souls which have been lost in the eyes of the world. They are the one order of the religious whose garments are of pure white. This is in token to their high calling and purity of life.[220]

On November 5, 1899, having made two years' novitiate, and taking the name Sister Mary of St. Helena, she solemnly professed her vows of religion for one year.[221] At the time, beside the three ordinary vows of poverty, chastity and obedience, the Sisters of the Good Shepherd took a fourth vow: to work for the conversion and instruction of "penitents." The vows were renewed annually, each November in Helen's case, for five years, before becoming perpetual.[222]

In March of 1900, Mother Loretto, the Missouri Provincial, went to Cuba to begin negotiations with the authorities to establish a house of the Good Shepherd in Havana as a reform school for girls.

> Many were the orphans and degraded poor after the cessation of hostilities, and the authorities at once established schools for every class, principal among these was the Reform School for Girls of Cuba, at Aldecoa. Anticipating the great need of such an institution, General Leonard Wood, Military Governor of the island of Cuba, conceived the idea of entrusting this pioneer work to the religious of the Good Shepherd, whose principal object in the religious life is to labor for the reformation of poor fallen women.[223]

The work of the Sisters in reclaiming fallen women was well known. The congregation had already established one house on the island in 1879. Bishop Sbarretti approved the plan and General Leonard Wood made all the arrangements. The building and furniture of this new house, known as The Reform School for Girls of Cuba, was government property and all expenses were to be defrayed by the government.[224] At the time, The finance minister serving in the military governor's cabinet was Pablo Desvernine y Galdós who became a friend to both Helen and Bishop Broderick.

When the school opened on July 15, 1900, it was staffed by eight sisters, including the young Sr. Mary of St. Helena, who arrived in Havana on May 14, 1900, and proceeded a few miles west to Aldecoa on May 27.[225] Eighteen months later she left the Congregation. In November of 1901, a date coinciding with her annual renewal of vows, she went to New York. "From that time until the day my mother died, Miss Bowlen lived with and cared for my mother," the bishop wrote in his notebook forty years later.[226]

The How and Why of Sr. Mary of St. Helena's Return to the World

The how and why of Sr. Mary of St. Helena's return to the world is open to speculation. When she arrived in Havana in 1900, she was twenty-one, newly professed, and in a foreign land. The reform school "was for some years a crown of thorns to the poor superiors and the Sisters who assisted in the work. At first the girls seemed absolutely uncontrollable, and the foreign language added to the Sisters' difficulties." [227]

Helen appears to have been a caring and helpful person, which may explain why she was sent to work at the school in Havana. Someone, Wood, or Desvernine, or Broderick himself, realized she was not up to the task, or she realized she was in the wrong setting for her own gifts. The temporary vows made it a much simpler matter for her to leave the Congregation. The bishop had recognized her talents and provided her a way out of the Congregation once she discerned it was not the vocation to which she was called.

Broderick was anticipating he would be sent to the Philippines. His aging mother's health and companionship was a concern to him, and the Philippines was a much greater distance from New York than Havana was from New York. In July of 1901, he went to St. Louis. His visit was covered by the St. Louis *Globe-Dispatch:* "Bonaventure Broderick of Havana was a guest at the Planters (Hotel). He will say mass this morning at the Convent of the Good Shepherd which provincial house has two branches in Havana under its jurisdiction."[228] Whether Sr. Mary of St. Helena was in St. Louis or Havana at the time is not known, but he may have travelled to Missouri to seek permission of the provincial for Sr. Mary of St. Helena to leave the congregation or at least to present her case for doing so; it is a plausible reason for his trip.

Four months later, she did not renew her annual vows. In November, at the end of her annual commitment, she went to Yonkers to care for Margaret Broderick. There is a note, written underneath her vows of 1899: "Sr. Mary of St. Helena returned to the world."[229]

He Sues a Magazine

In June of 1912, the *Kingston Daily Freeman* reported "Bishop B.F. Broderick is spending a few days in Boston." The trip to Boston may have been to see a lawyer because he soon fired the first shot in a drawn-out battle of well-publicized lawsuits. This one involved a magazine article published in 1910 that included an assault on his reputation. He filed a claim of defamation of character against Pearson's Magazine, a publication known for its socialist leanings.

The case garnered national attention and the *Times-Democrat* of New Orleans carried the story on its July 1 front page under the bold headline "SLANDER CHARGE MADE BY PRIEST:"

> The Rev. Dr. Bonaventure Broderick, formerly a professor in St. Thomas Catholic Seminary, Hartford. Conn., and more recently at the Church of the Holy Angels, in Havana, Cuba, today brought suit in the Supreme Court to recover $100,000 damages for alleged defamation of character. He has named as defendant a magazine which published an article, "The Man Who Owns Cuba."[230] This article dealt particularly with the career in Cuba of Frank Steinhart. It was written by Robert Wickliffe Woolley and talked about picturesque chapters in the life of Steinhart in his rise from a clerk in the American army to his position as "owner" of Cuba.[231]

The article that irritated Broderick contained the following paragraph:

The first bit of buccaneering—that is the most appropriate name for such an operation—attempted by Steinhart was when he entered into a deal with Juan Antonio Frias and Father Buenna Ventura Broderick to sell the old monastery down on the harbor front of Havana and certain other church property to the Cuban government for $2,036,000. (Steinhart) was then Chief Clerk to the Military Government. Governor-General Wood took an option at that price. It may be only a coincidence that the Presidential elections of 1900 were about to occur; in Havana, Cubans said then, and they say now, that the administration at Washington took this option because it was not deemed desirable to run any chances of antagonizing such a powerful organization as the Roman Catholic church. It subsequently developed that the church was to receive only $1,000,000 of the purchase price, the remainder going to Steinhart, Frias, and Broderick as a commission for making the sale. William F. Redding, a wealthy American who went to Havana a poor boy more than fifty years ago and who has done much to promote a kindly feeling between the Yankees, Cubans, and Spaniards, heard of the deal and informed Bishop Estrada of Havana that it would not be necessary to pay a commission to anyone. So great was the scandal provoked by this attempted transaction, that several years later, Mr. Redding, who is a Papal Count and Marquis, reported Broderick's part in the transaction to Rome. By that time, Broderick, who was the rector of the Church of the Holy Angels in Havana, had been created a Monsignor and titular bishop. The result was that this speculative priest was suspended from all offices, and he now resides in New York without a charge.[232]

Redding died several months before the lawsuit. He died a rich man; the wealthiest American in Cuba, according to his obituary in the *Washington Post* on December 30, 1911:

> Count William Redding, aged sixty-seven, a man well known here and also to many Americans, was found dead in a bathroom of the Hotel Inglaterra. Fifty-seven years ago, the late Archbishop Hughes of New York came to Havana on a diocesan visit. He brought with him William Redding, who was a poor boy of ten. The boy remained here and in time became the richest and foremost American in Cuba. As a recognition of his great work for charity and his services to the Roman Catholic church the late Pope Leo XIII made him a Knight of St. Gregory and later raised him to the dignity of a papal count.[233]

The offending magazine article must have produced yet another episode of *déjà vu* for Broderick, harking back to the allegation of conspiracy between Steinhart, Frias, and Broderick that was one of the grievous accusations Chapelle had made in 1904.

If Redding, well connected to the Church as he was, did report the alleged Steinhart-Frias-Broderick scheme to Rome as the magazine claimed, he may have done so, not directly, but through Chapelle, who was so incensed that he made the long, arduous trip to Rome in 1904 to accuse Broderick. With great irony, it is notable that Steinhart's appointment as Chief Clerk to the Military Government was endorsed by Chapelle who telegrammed seven words to President Roosevelt on January 22, 1903: "Think proposed appointment of Steinhart very appropriate."[234]

Broderick's suit against the magazine brought him some relief as Pearson's printed a *mea culpa* in its May 1913 issue:

> During the summer of 1910 we published in connection with an article entitled "The Man Who Owns Cuba" certain statements about the Right Rev. Bishop Broderick to which he objected. Having been convinced of the investigation that we have made that the bishop's objections are justified we make this *amende honorable*.[235]

Whether he received a financial settlement in addition to the public contrition is not known, but the publisher of Pearson's filed for bankruptcy in 1917 listing its liabilities as $100,000.[236]

Friction with David

From his home at Villa Marguerite in Saugerties, Bishop Broderick wrote to his brother in Cienfuegos where David was on site concluding the construction project.[237] The letter, dated January 12, 1912, is friendly, but focused on finances, and an undercurrent of anxiety is discernable.

He included two bills, "one for money expended on account of Donovan & Philips and one for personal services." He explains his expenses on behalf for Donovan & Phillips: "Almost every day for months and months I was obliged to go to N.Y. City and spent money on R.R. tickets, car fare, telephone calls, and restaurant and hotel bills."

For personal services he tries to balance the ledger between himself and co-owner, John Sullivan. "My object in rendering a bill for personal services is to have an offset to the $5,000.00 charge that S. is making for professional services. I feel that I was obliged to give much more time and personal attention to the business than he was, and that I am quite as worthy of my hire as he."

He expected to receive not only the amounts outlined, but also his share of the profits from the contract: "The Judge told me he felt certain the Government would make final payment this month. What do you think?"

There is no record of David's reply, if any, but the final payment of $557,667 was received by David a few months later;[238] but the amount he passed along to the bishop and to Sullivan was far less than the two expected, thus triggering the litigation that followed.

The Sewer System Explodes

In the summer of 1913, the bishop and Sullivan take legal action against David in a suit for $75,000. Theirs is one of several lawsuits that will emerge involving the "Cienfuegos aqueduct contract," a contract valued at $3,800,000.[239]

> The action is based on a certain contract which had been executed with the government of Cuba for the building of a water and sewerage system at Cienfuegos, the work having been completed by Rev. Dr. Broderick and Mr. Sullivan, as sub-contractors under the firm name of Donovan & Phillips. While the two systems were under construction in Cienfuegos, David F. Broderick was the representative in Cuba for Donovan & Phillips.[240]

David insisted he not only paid his brother and Sullivan all they were entitled but had overpaid them by more than $20,000. He filed a counterclaim asking that he be awarded $75,000.[241]

Because David was a Connecticut resident, the case came before Connecticut Superior Court Judge Marcus Holcomb in Hartford. Bishop Broderick spent an entire day of the trial on the witness stand explaining to the court how he became involved in the project, but he first answered a Hartford journalist who quizzed him about his connection with the Church. In the conversation Broderick, according to the reporter, gave the impression that he is still connected to the Peter's Pence collection, but lacking specified duties:

> He was in court all day. He is much stouter than he was a few years ago, when he was connected with the Hartford Roman Catholic diocese. After leaving here he was auxiliary Roman Catholic bishop of Havana, Cuba, and he is now titular bishop of Juliopolis, but it is not necessary for him to have a residence in Juliopolis (Asia Minor). In fact, he said to a *Courant* reporter, there is a tacit understanding that the titular bishops do not exercise their authority of bishop. By virtue of his office of bishop, in Roman Catholicism he is a Prince of the Church, and he said that the church in which he officiates is his chapel at his home in Saugerties. In the church in America, he has the office of commander general for the collection of the Peter's Pence. The intention of the office had been, Bishop Broderick said, to create inspiration for the Peter's Pence, but just after he was appointed, a few years ago, he received directions from Rome not to become active in the office until further orders were received by him. He has not since received any further orders, although continuing to hold the office of commander general, and he said that, within a few years, the annual Peter's Pence had increased from about $80,000 to over $300,000.[242]

On the witness stand he was asked to show the cause and the way he severed his activities in the Church and in the Diocese of Hartford. He made it clear that he is still in good standing and in answer to a question about his position in the Church, Broderick replied "once a bishop in the Catholic Church, always a bishop."[243]

He said he first met Reilly in 1900 in Cuba when Reilly called on him with letters of introduction from two New Yorkers, John D. Crimmins and U.S. Senator T.C. Platt, but his first business with Reilly came in 1906. It was then that Reilly was the general contractor for the Cienfuegos project and asked Broderick to help find Italian immigrants to work on the sewer system construction. The project stalled with the civil unrest of 1907 in Cuba. In 1908 Reilly again approached Broderick for help recruiting laborers, placing no restrictions on nationality. This is when he met the subcontractors, Simon Donovan and George Philipps who suggested to him that his brother David might be employed by their firm. The bishop shared an anecdote from the witness stand that foretold the breakup of Messrs. Donovan and Phillips:

> Finally, Donovan and Phillips got to quarreling and Reilly complained as to the way the work was going. Finally, the bishop said, he was told that, in a quarrel Donovan and Phillips had, one threw an inkwell at the other and after a conference between the (bishop) and Reilly and the sub-contractors, David Broderick was named as a referee to settle the disputes between Donovan and Phillips.[244]

The two were not strangers to controversy. In 1905, Donovan, as contractor, and Phillips as Superintendent of Sewers in

Boston, were embroiled in the so called "Fenway Scandal" that resulted in a grand jury investigation into the costs associated with construction of sewers in that section of Boston. No criminal charges were filed, but Phillips resigned his post early in 1906.

In 1909 Donovan and Phillips finally gave up on the business and Broderick and John A. Sullivan, the former Massachusetts congressman who was also a lawyer familiar with both Simon Donovan and George Phillips, stepped in and assumed the company, liabilities and all, keeping the name Donovan & Phillips Co. with the bishop as the majority owner.[245] They hired David Broderick as the general manager, and Reilly's son, Hugh Reilly, Jr., known as "Hughey," as superintendent of accounts and claims.

On the stand Broderick shared that the elder Reilly showed him letters written by Hughey that implied it was the younger man's intent to supplant the elders as subcontractors; the bishop communicated this to David who responded that the bishop had "judged young Reilly harshly as he was all right and in position to assist or hurt the firm." David told him that Hughey was coming to New York and David recommended the bishop "buy Reilly a ring and be nice to him."

> The bishop said he took (Hughey) to Tiffany's and bought him a ring and Reilly thanked him for it. Reilly told him that David had complained that the bishop had not been as kind to (David) as he had been to some, and the bishop said that Reilly told him that he thought that the bishop should be more generous with (David).

This led the bishop to make an offer of added compensation to both David and Hughey if they would stay in Cuba, work together, and complete the project.[246] They did and in 1912 the final payment was made, and when David returned from Cuba, the bishop met him in Hartford:

> He asked David where the money was. David said he had it all right and when the bishop asked him how much, he said he and young Reilly had jointly collected $558,000. David didn't want to talk to him about it and told him he had a mercenary mind. He could not find how much David had and his brother told him that the money was in drafts in the safe at the Waldorf Astoria in New York.
> He told David that he should not have drafts in his own name, as the money belonged to Donovan & Phillips. There had been a long fight for it (with the government), the bishop said he told David. He told him that he might get killed in an automobile accident, or in some other way, and, if that happened his estate might claim the money and the bishop told him that would mean another fight for it.
> Finally, he told David to think the matter over. The bishop said he left his brother to go to the Garde.[247] He invited David to have breakfast with him at the Garde the next morning. David said he would, but he did not reach the hotel.[248]

Ironically, during the trial, it was Bonaventure, not David, who was in an automobile accident when the brakes failed and he was injured, though not seriously, in a "runaway" near Saugerties.[249]

The judge made a decision in August that satisfied no one. Judge Holcomb found that Bishop Broderick and Sullivan were entitled to recover $17,000 from David. Not happy, the two gave notice of appeal to the Supreme Court. Disappointed as well, David also filed an appeal.[250]

More than a year later, as 1914 came to a close, and before the case reached the Supreme Court, Reilly and the brothers reconciled their differences out of court and dropped their appeals. The Hartford *Courant* published the good news on January 1, 1915, under the headline "Happy New Year for Brodericks."

> David F. Broderick of Farmington and his brother, Bishop Bonaventure F. Broderick of Saugerties, N. Y., who, at one time, was connected with the Roman Catholic diocese of Hartford, have settled all of the differences in which they were antagonistic to each other, it was learned yesterday. As this necessarily implies all of the litigation in which they were on different sides has been dropped, and the bishop and his brother who had been on the "outs" for a considerable time, are in friendly relations, it was indicated yesterday.[251]

A third legal action, also begun in 1913 and tied to the Cienfuegos sewer project was more drawn out. This suit against the Broderick brothers, Reilly, Sr. and his son, and Sullivan was brought by Jose Antonio Frias, the former Cuban senator and one time mayor of Cienfuegos, and party to the alleged Steinhart-Frias-Broderick million-dollar real estate commission scheme of 1904. This time it was Frias who was bitter.

In announcing the case, newspapers made Bishop Broderick the focus of the suit. The *Evening Enterprise* of Poughkeepsie,

More Turmoil: Gossip & Legal Drama, 1912–1915   95

NY led with the headline "Make Bishop the Defendant in $750,000 Lawsuit":

> Charging conspiracy and fraud, an action for $750,000 damages was begun today against David Broderick and his wife, of Hartford; Bishop Bonaventure Broderick, of Saugerties, N. Y., John A. Sullivan, of Boston, formerly representative in Congress; Hugh J. Reilly and Hugh J. Reilly, Jr., of New York City. The action is brought by Jose Antonio Frias, of Havana, Cuba, and New York, in the name of the Latin American Contracting and Improvement Company, which is his assignee. It grows out of the $3,800,000 sewer and water system built in Cienfuegos, Cuba, from 1908 to 1910. Hugh J. Reilly, of New York, was the general contractor and there were several subcontractors, including Donovan & Philips, of Boston; Bishop Broderick and Mr. Sullivan, who bought the Donovan and Philips interests.[252]

Frias alleged that Reilly, Sr., had made an agreement on behalf of the Donovan & Phillips Co. to pay him a percentage of the money received from the Cuban government on account of the contract. He said that he assigned the contract to the Latin American Contracting and Improvement Co.

Frias withdrew his suit in March of 1915 without consideration,[253] but sued Reilly separately. In turn Reilly sued Frias, leading to the arrest of Frias on allegations of forging Reilly's name to contracts.

The Governor of New York is Impeached

Broderick did not escape the limelight of the Frias-Reilly legal fracas. In an odd collision of circumstance and court calendars, the arrest of Frias drew Broderick into another high-profile case:

the 1913 trial of impeachment against the recently elected governor of New York, William Sulzer, a former Congressman who served in Washington from 1895 to 1912. The Sulzer trial was complicated by accusations of conspiracy involving the political machine Tammany Hall and its leader Charles Murphy.

Frias made disclosures to the effect that Sulzer, while a member of Congress, had conducted illegal negotiations on behalf of Reilly in Cuba with the State Department.[254]

Broderick was dragged into to the controversy because of his relationship with both Reilly and Sulzer. He had earlier voiced concerns about Sulzer's integrity and tried to prevent him from running for governor, even predicting impeachment would soon follow if he won; in that effort he offered details of Sulzer to Congress.

> As a result of his long and intimate association with Hugh J. Reilly's Cuban contracting firm during the period when it was charged William Sulzer was promoting its interests from the vantage point of his position on the Military Affairs and Foreign Relations Committees of the House of Representatives, the Rt. Rev. Bonaventure F. Broderick, a Roman Catholic Bishop, has accumulated data which he said yesterday he would be willing to lay before a Congressional committee of investigation.
>
> During the campaign when he became convinced that Mr. Sulzer probably would be elected governor Bishop Broderick predicted to several of Mr. Sulzer's friends that impeachment surely would follow his election.
>
> Bishop Broderick says that his frequent contact with Mr. Sulzer during the period when the Reilly claims were being forwarded convinced him so completely that

Mr. Sulzer ought not to be governor of New York that he laid the data he is now willing to present to a congressional investigating committee, before Mr. Sulzer himself, before the state department, and before the department of Justice.[255]

The *New York Times* carried the above on its front-page under the bold headline "Sulzer A Tool, Says Broderick," but the bishop, with pastoral sensitivity, noted his concern was borne of charity, and concluding with a nod to Shakespeare's *King Lear* was quoted, "I feel very sorry about what has happened. What I say of Sulzer I want to say in a kindly spirit for he has been more sinned against than sinning. By that I mean he was used by men more clever than he, who used him to throw him aside and deceive him."[256]

What he said about Sulzer, and what Shakespeare's King Lear said about himself, could also have been said about the exiled bishop: that he was a man more sinned against than sinning.[257]

Sulzer's political career was on the ropes and the desperate governor, through a surrogate, had typewritten statements handed out to the newspapermen gathered in the audience room of a Capitol building suite occupied by the governor. The surrogate was James G. Garrison, assistant to John Hennessy, Sulzer's political manager. After handing out the statement Garrison quickly exited through a door to a private room occupied by Sulzer.

The unsigned statement was a litany of attacks against several Sulzer political opponents, most of whom surfaced during what Sulzer labelled "the Murphy conspiracy." The typewritten statement included the following accusation:

> The unfrocked Bishop Broderick who has been telling a weird tale to The New York Times about the Frias claim and who also may be indicted for his share in the Murphy conspiracy against the Governor, Broderick was driven out of the Church of Rome for corruption in Havana where he was bishop and is now living openly at Saugerties with a nun he stole from a convent near St Louis. Cardinals Farley and Gibbons can tell about Broderick and what crimes he committed in Cuba.[258]

Broderick was not "unfrocked," but he was "living openly with a woman." She was, of course, Helen Bowlen, his mother's companion, and caretaker. At least the statement handed out by Garrison fell short of the "married" rumor Cardinal Farley had investigated a year earlier.

True to Broderick's prediction, Sulzer was governor only 289 days. Accused of campaign finance corruption, including filing false statements of receipts and expenditures in the election campaign of 1912, misusing monies contributed for his campaign, illegally converting campaign contributions, and corruptly influencing the stock exchange, he was impeached in August, convicted, and removed from office in October of 1913.[259]

After Sulzer's impeachment, the Frias-Reilly debacle dragged on in courtrooms until April 1914 when the Supreme Court decided in favor of Reilly.

With Cuba and its drawn-out drama behind him, Broderick moved on to the next chapter of his life and more tranquil years in his cherished Hudson River Valley. In May of 1914 he sold Villa Marguerite to Judge Lyman Warren.[260] The *Kingston Daily Freeman* reported on the sale with a nod to the bishop's generosity:

> Bishop Broderick on Saturday sold his estate "Margaret Villa," at Saugerties to Judge Warren of New York, who has taken possession. The bishop has removed to New York. He will be greatly missed in Saugerties as many people in that village can testify to his many acts of kindness and philanthropy which was always done in an unostentatious manner. There was never a Christmas since he went to Saugerties, but he liberally provided for the larders of the poorer families of the village and vicinity.[261]

He may have removed to New York briefly, to an apartment he kept on West 170th Street, but he soon bought a place not far from Villa Marguerite, down the hill from Barclay Heights in the village of Saugerties, at 70 Main Street, a home once known as the Lasher mansion, where his mother quietly lived out her remaining years, cared for by Helen Bowlen.

8. Quiet Times, 1915–1926

Broderick was an automobile enthusiast long before he opened his gas station. When living he Yonkers he had his 1910 Stanley Steamer and in 1916 he owned a gasoline-powered Franklin automobile. The top-of-the-line Franklin, the Series 9A Touring model, sold for around $2,000. He displayed his "handsome five passenger" car at an automobile show in Poughkeepsie in February[262] and again at Roxmor Colony, a celebrated retreat resort in the Catskill Mountains at Woodland, about thirty miles west of Saugerties.[263]

The First World War

These were the years preceding the First World War when Europe was embroiled in turmoil and the United States remained neutral. The patience of America ran out on April 6, 1917, when President Woodrow Wilson signed the resolution declaring war with the Imperial Germany Government.

The bishop and Helen Bowlen immediately joined the Red Cross Auxiliary of Saugerties.[264] The civic-minded bishop, now forty-eight, helped form a Saugerties committee whose mission in support of the war focused on "proper patriotic spirit, respect for the flag, recruits and recruiting, statistics and census, prevention of extravagance, and the elimination waste and larger use of agricultural lands and efficiency thereon." [265] Other members of the Ulster County Home Defense Committee included John T. Washburn of the brickmaking family, attorney Frederick E. W. Darrow, mayor William Ziegler, banker John A. Snyder, and Martin Cantine,[266] whose family-owned paper processing company supplied slick and glossy paper used at the time by magazines *Vanity Fair* and *Vogue*, and later *The New Yorker*.[267]

Within days the committee, led by Broderick and Cantine, sent a telegram of support to President Wilson:

> The citizens of the town of Saugerties, New York assembled in public meeting have unanimously endorsed your message to Congress, and to express to you their thanks and appreciation of the courage and straightforwardness you have exemplified to the people of this nation and other countries in what we believe to be true Americanism, hold ourselves in readiness to do our part in any way it may be your pleasure to command.[268]

A major accomplishment of the committee was the launch of a summer "training camp" located at Black House Point on Lake Champlain in North Hero, Vermont. Broderick, whose name was on the deed, assumed management of the camp known as the Ethan Allen Training Camp.[269] The camp was well staffed, including Henry Monteith, Broderick's former high school teacher; Major George Chandler, a surgeon and first superintendent of the New York State Police, and Brigadier General William Verbeck, former Commander of the New York National Guard.

The *New York Times* announced the opening of the camp:

> A booklet of information concerning Ethan Allen Training Camp for boys was issued yesterday from the

camp's executive and recruiting office at 154 Fifth Avenue. The camp will open on July 1 on North Hero Island, Lake Champlain. and run for two months, and the instruction will include both military training and educational lectures on good citizenship. Physical training, sports and recreations will also be fostered. General William Verbeck, President of St John's School, Manlius, N. Y. will be Superintendent and Military Commander of the camp; Major George Chandler of Kingston, N.Y. will be in charge of the medical and sanitary department, and Professor Henry R. Monteith of the Connecticut Agricultural College, will direct the lectures and entertainment.

The *Times* also carried advertisements for the camp:

ETHAN ALLEN TRAINING CAMP
FOR BOYS 14-21
Intensive Military Training by Army Officers and
West Point Cadets
New regiment is being formed for five weeks intensive
training July 2nd-Sept. 1st.
Maintenance and Instruction $100. Address Brig. Gen.
Wm. Verbeck, North Hero Island, Vt.[270]

The program received a strong endorsement from Martin H. Glynn, journalist, orator and statesman, a former congressman and governor of New York, who wrote Broderick, "I do not believe any young man could spend two months in your Camp and follow its course of training without greatly benefited in mind, in body, in patriotic devotion, and in ability to serve his country in time of need."[271]

His Mother's Death

As America was entering the war, Margaret Broderick's health was failing. On July 5, 1917, she died at age 87 at their home on Main Street in Saugerties. Years later, near the end of his life, Broderick, in his unstable hand, in a notebook, recorded the scene of his mother's death:

> Two days before her death my mother lapsed into a comatose condition. Summoned by telegraph from a distance of about four hundred miles I traveled by automobile day and night until I reached her bedside. Almost immediately my mother regained consciousness, opened her eyes and greeted me lovingly. Helen was kneeling on one side of the bed. Turning to Miss Bowlen, she thanked her for her long years of affectionate care to her, told her what a kind and dutiful son I had always been, assuring her that I had never caused her any sorrow, and asked Miss Bowlen to care for me as carefully as she had for her. Then turning to me she exacted a promise from me that I would always protect and care for "Helen." This promise I cheerfully and sincerely gave. Within an hour my mother's soul left this earth for its home in Heaven.[272]

The *Hartford Courant* carried her obituary, noting that death came at four in the morning. The funeral Mass was held at St. Mary's Church, Saugerties on July 6 and interment followed in Mt. St. Benedict Cemetery in Hartford.

Helen Bowlen stayed on as Bishop Broderick's housekeeper.

The next several years, despite the war, were serene for Broderick as he travelled between Saugerties and Lake Saranac, Montreal, and North Hero, Vermont where, in August of 1917 he built a "cozy little summer home a few rods north of the Ethan Allen Camp."[273]

In the fall of 1920, he helped rescue two Belgian army officers whose hot air balloon ran out of steam and crashed. The balloon, entered in an international race, had taken flight in Birmingham, Alabama. The two had been in the air for forty hours when they found themselves falling to the earth over Lake Champlain with no life preservers. The basket hit the water about one mile from shore. Fortunately, a strong west wind blew them ashore. Broderick rushed to the scene in his automobile and the two were wrapped in blankets and taken to the Ethan Allen Camp to recover.[274]

A Letter to the Editor

Fifteen years removed from active ministry the bishop maintained a sense for the pastoral and respect for the power of the pen. He wrote a Letter to the Editor of the *New York Times* expressing his concern over growing anti-Semitism in America resulting from the publication of a pamphlet known as "The Protocols."

Originating in czarist Russia in the nineteenth century, "The Protocols of the Elders of Zion" was an anti-Semitic pamphlet that, in summary, claimed to be minutes of twenty-four meetings held in secret by Jewish leaders plotting to control the world by taking control of international institutions, including the media.

In 1920 the pamphlet, published as "The Protocols and World Revolution" by Small, Maynard & Company of Boston, was gaining traction in the United States. Author Briggit Sion, an international expert in the fields of museums and memorials, provides this background:

> The text makes the Jews responsible for present and past disasters, from the downfall of Christian monarchies to the French Revolution and the advancement of liberal and bourgeois ideas. The Protocols contain a number of metaphors essential to conspiracy vocabulary, such as an "invisible hand" pushing pieces on a chessboard. The plotters are portrayed as poisonous snakes, spiders weaving their webs, and wolves ready to devour Christian sheep. The last protocols describe the future reign of the Jews in Christian terms, announcing the coming of a "King of the Jews" who will be "the real Pope of the Universe, the patriarch of an international Church."[275]

Broderick's letter was triggered by a December 1 article in the *New York Times* reporting that the pamphlet had been denounced by a conference of leading Jewish organizations as a "base forgery" and as a "recrudescence of medieval bigotry and stupidity."[276] The *Times* published his letter on December 16:

> Please permit me to express through the columns of your newspaper my abhorrence of the anti-Jewish campaign now being conducted in this country. Surely this attempt to stir up race and religious prejudices will meet with the failure it so richly deserves.
>
> I have carefully examined the "protocols" upon which the calumnies against the Jews are now being based, and I unhesitatingly pronounce these documents spurious and entirely unworthy of consideration. Moreover, I believe the statement made about the connection

of Jews with the Russian revolution and with radical movements in this and other countries to be incorrect.

Our civilization owes much of its beginnings to the Jewish race. If what the Jews contributed to it were taken away little would be left. History shows the Jews to always have been a constructive and not a destructive force. They are patient, industrious and thrifty. They make good citizens, and their family life is exemplary. They are kind and generous to the helpless of their own race and their philanthropy extends to all humanity.

As a sincere admirer of the Jewish people for their many excellent qualities of head and heart, I take pleasure in assuring them that it is my belief that they will not suffer in the esteem of the American public because of the unfair attacks to which they are being subjected.[277]

The letter, signed, "Bonaventure F. Broderick, Titular Bishop of Juliopolis," was well-received in the Jewish community and reprinted in the December issue of *The American Hebrew* along with a letter praising Broderick written by jurist, judge, and poet John Jerome Rooney.[278] The two letters appeared under the headline "Bishop Broderick says 'Protocols' Unworthy of Consideration."

Several months later, Philip Graves, a correspondent of *The Times of London*, exposed the "Protocols" as "having largely been plagiarized from an 1864 book attacking the regime of Emperor Napoleon III of France. The original book took the form of an imagined dialogue between the philosophers Machiavelli and Montesquieu."[279] The *New York Times* devoted an entire page to the Graves exposé on Sept. 4, 1921, with the banner headline "Proof that the Jewish Protocols were Forged."[280]

After his letter to the *Times* Broderick began to use "Titular Bishop of Juliopolis" less, while favoring "Doctor Broderick" in the academic sense, implying he may have lost hope of ever reconciling with the Church.

The Lake Champlain Vacation Camp

After the war Broderick and Martin Cantine converted the Ethan Allen Training Camp to a vacation camp. In 1921 Cantine purchased the camp, and the bishop became the manager of the fifty-two-acre Lake Champlain Vacation Camp.[281]

Active despite growing health concerns he continued to travel between New York, Saugerties, and North Hero. The local papers in Vermont seemed interested in tracing his movements with short reports such as "Dr. Broderick has returned to New York City after spending a few days" in North Hero.[282] In 1926 Broderick turned over management of the camp to Mr. Charles E. Tudhope.[283]

In 1925 he sold the house on Main Street in Saugerties and while maintaining an apartment on West 170th Street in New York City, moved east from Saugerties across the Hudson to Dutchess County, first to 32 Parker Avenue in Poughkeepsie[284] and then to the hamlet of Washington Hollow near Millbrook. Washington Hollow was one of three hamlets that made up the village of Pleasant Valley; the others are Pleasant Valley and Salt Point. At first, he was the subject of curiosity and even an oddball rumor that he was running a hot dog stand, but he was eventually embraced by the Dutchess County community as he was in Saugerties. In the years that followed he became a columnist for a local newspaper, was in demand as a public speaker, and opened his little auto accessory and gasoline business.

After twenty years of silence from Rome, Dr. Broderick could be forgiven for thinking that any living friends he may have in the Church hierarchy had forgotten him. If he thought so, he was wrong. Several old friends did remember him, and wheels were turning, slowly and at a great distance, but turning they were, in his direction.

9. A Phantom Hot Dog Stand and the Fabled Gas Station, 1926–1939

The Move to Washington Hollow

Why the move to Washington Hollow? The question was put to Edna Tyldsley by seminarian Thomas Ginty in 1989 when drafting his master's thesis. Edna knew Broderick well during the 1930's, telling Ginty "he was considered part of the family." Edna was the wife of John Tyldsley, editor and publisher of the *Millbrook Round Table*, a weekly newspaper published in the nearby town of Millbrook. She suggested that the bishop may have been offered a position at the newspaper by her father-in-law, William Tyldsley, the founder of the paper. William, who started publishing the paper in 1906, retired in 1930 and moved to Texas, leaving the business to Edna's husband, John, who edited and published the paper until his death in 1960. Broderick began writing for the paper in the mid-1930's.

Real estate records show a sale in 1926 of seventy acres of land along Washington Hollow Road to Helen Bowlen from the heirs of Webster Knickerbocker. The centerpiece of the property was a ten-room farmhouse sitting on a hill above Washington Hollow Road, a home with a considerable view of the vicinity. Several years later, Broderick opened his gas station and auto accessory business on the highway below the house.

The Phantom Hot Dog Stand

In 1929, after three years in the area rumors began circulating about this mysterious man. Was he or was he not affiliated with the Catholic Church? One rumor that made it into the press claimed he was running a hot dog stand—this one he denied in the strongest terms when asked by the *Poughkeepsie Eagle-News*.

> Hot dog stand! Certainly not! I do not run a hot dog stand or any other kind of stand. That is the product of the imagination of some newspaperman. Those young fellows write principally from their imaginations, I guess. It will be remarkable if we ever see youth and brains together! [285]

To complicate matters, Monsignor Joseph Sheahan, dean of the Poughkeepsie area parishes told the *Eagle-News* that Broderick had no connection with the archdiocese, saying "He is not under my supervision. He is a visitor here as far as the Church is concerned."[286]

The Poughkeepsie paper was relentless:

> Bishop Broderick has lived at Washington Hollow a number of years. He has become acquainted with many persons living near him and has become an established member of the community. Stories of the former bishop of Havana living in seclusion in a wayside farmhouse at Washington Hollow and conducting a hot dog stand led many to ask why a clergyman was living apart, apparently having no connection with the church. [287]

Broderick soon had enough of the silliness and decided to set the record straight, telling the paper: "The reason for that is that people do not understand the organization of our church. They think that because a clergyman does not preach every Sunday and have a church that he is unattached. There is a difference between a bishop and a parish priest, you know. I am certainly not unattached. I am connected with the diplomatic service of the church."

His reference to diplomatic service is another sign that he was holding on, in some way, emotionally, to the ill-fated Peter's Pence mission of 1905, much like the entry he submitted for the 1909 *Who's Who*, and his mention of it from the witness stand in the 1913 lawsuit against his brother.

Not surprisingly, gossip circulated that he had lost his ecclesiastical privileges. Father Edmund Harty, pastor of St. Mary's Church in Saugerties, put that rumor to rest in short order, telling those who inquired, that Broderick celebrated Mass daily in a private chapel in his home.[288]

The Depression Years and his Gas Station

The 1929 scuttlebutt about Broderick preceded the stock market crash of October 29 and the panic selling that foreshadowed the Great Depression. There is no evidence that Broderick had significant stock market investments; he was more interested in real estate. No one knows the exact year he began his business of selling automobile accessories and gasoline on the property, but 1935 seems likely.

What inspired Broderick to open a gas station? In addition to being an automobile enthusiast he may have begun to feel the effects of the global financial decline. He began to divest himself of real estate he held in the Bronx, including two five-story tenements on 3rd Avenue, selling one in 1933[289] and another in 1938.[290] He also dispensed with property on Colgate Avenue.[291] Beginning in October of 1931 and continuing through December of 1934 he was the plaintiff in several lawsuits against real estate developers, banks, and mortgage companies.

Beginning in the 1920's detached structures built for the sale of gasoline began to appear to meet the demand generated by the Ford Model T and other affordable automobiles. In the first race to expand, companies and independent operators constructed basic sheds to serve as drive-in filling stations. Many were rudimentary frame shacks with wood or corrugated metal exteriors.[292]

By the 1930's they were more well-defined: a small building with gas pumps in front. But stations also offered supplies, tires, batteries, and oil and simple services like tire patching. In 1920, America had 15,000 gas stations, and by 1930, over 100,000.[293]

It seems unlikely that he would install his gas pumps along Washington Hollow Road in the early 1930's when unemployment began to rise from 5% before the crash to 17% in 1931 and 22% in 1934.[294] His inspiration may have come from the increased traffic due to the 1935 opening of the Eastern State Parkway (now the Taconic Parkway) into southern Dutchess County where construction continued through 1939. The highway intersects with Washington Hollow Road (now US Route 44) just west of his gas station.[295] The Parkway made access to the road to Millbrook easier for wealthy New Yorkers who owned rural properties in the area to enjoy on weekends and during vacations.[296] Kevin DeMartine, whose mother, Evelyn Mabie, bought the bishop's gas station from Helen Bowlen in

1941, believes that Broderick's pumps were among the first along Washington Hollow Road after the Parkway opened.[297] How much time he spent at the business, and whether he worked it personally or simply oversaw the operation, is not known. By 1939 he had turned over the operation to someone else and the station was for sale with an asking price of $20,000.[298]

The Millbrook Round Table

In the mid-1930's he began writing for the *Millbrook Round Table*. His column was titled "Things, Events, and Men," and he had free rein to write on a wide range of subjects. His topics included poetry and poets, politics and politicians, labor strife and unions, gardening, British royalty, automobiles, education, and the weather.

In an October 1938 column titled "Splendid Among the Ruins" he used the impact of a hurricane as a bridge to laud the poet Emily Dickinson.

> The hurricane that uprooted a few trees hereabouts was but a gentle breeze compared to the force of the wind that wrought havoc through the Connecticut River valley. One of the most seriously damaged of all the beautiful old towns for which that part of our country is noted, was Amherst, Massachusetts.
>
> Here, more than a hundred years ago, Samuel Fowler Dickinson laid deep and solid the foundations of Amherst College. For a lifetime, the son of this apostle of education, Edward Dickinson, watched over and caused to grow the work so well begun by his self-sacrificing parent.

> Second among the three children of Edward Dickinson was Emily Dickinson who is steadily and surely being placed on the pedestal of recognition she deserves—that of the greatest of lyric poets of any age. In this, the field of intellectual achievement in which woman has most excelled, she stands supreme.[299]

The same year Dr. Broderick used his pen to heap praise on Anthony Eden, who, seventeen years later, succeeded Winston Churchill as prime minister of the United Kingdom.

> In New England when I was a boy one of the most complimentary things that could be said about a man is "he is every inch a gentleman." How aptly this old-fashioned expression applies to Anthony Eden, the recent Minister for Foreign Affairs in England, who came to our shore a few days ago to be a guest in this country for a week or two.
>
> Everything about him is admirable—his size and figure, his looks, his age, his manners, his tact, his political record in England, and the speech which he came to our shores to make.
>
> This speech proved to be particularly gratifying, for, guided by precedent, many thoughtful and patriotic citizens of the nation, feared it was to be merely a terrifying blast of English propaganda. As it was delivered, it was the very best of taste.
>
> Lifting, therefore, my imaginary hollow-stemmed goblet, I here propose the toast: "Here's to Anthony Eden who by his every act and his entire attitude while he has been our guest has proved to us and has the shown the whole world that he is every inch a gentleman."[300]

His concerns extended to labor unions, opposing their policies here and abroad, as in this piece from 1938.

> The unreasonable demands of the French Labor Unions, and particularly their insistence on a Forty Hour Week threatened that country with a general strike last week that was averted only by the use of the army to police duty.
>
> It is a wonder that the plight to which Labor Unions have brought France does not awaken our rabble-rousing politicians to a sense of the danger that they are bringing, by the same means, upon our nation.[301]

A sampling of other columns includes "Love of Country," "The Milk-Marketing Situation," "The Social Security Decision," and "The Evian Conference." His interest included British royalty, writing a 1937 column regarding "The Coronation in London of King George VI".[302] Helen Bowlen also held a similar interest, writing a letter to the New York *Times* in 1936 chastising the editor for his misuse of the title "premier Earl of England."[303]

Broderick not only opposed unions, but also Dutchess County native Franklin D. Roosevelt who was elected president in 1932, taking office on March 4, 1933. He took FDR to task many times in his column. If one wonders how this played with the local readership, it played well, considering Roosevelt never won his home county, or neighboring Ulster County.

Did he ever discuss Cuba? "He would from time to time make reference to his stay in Cuba but only in very general terms," Edna Tyldsley said. In one of his columns Broderick reminisces about a man he met in Cuba, Captain Lucien Young, who was, at the time, the harbormaster of the Port of Havana.[304]

Edna said he "was a very self-effacing and compassionate individual who took enjoyment in making his wine and tending to his own business,"[305] adding that "Doctor Broderick was a well-educated, highly motivated, articulate and sensitive gentleman who loved to be around people" [306] and a "charismatic individual who spread the Gospel in a non-clerical way. There was no need for him to preach the Gospel, he lived it."[307]

The present author corresponded with Edna's son, J. Ogden Tyldsley, Jr., who recalls from his earliest memory that a large silver mounted photograph of Broderick "dressed in full regalia" stood prominently in the Tyldsley living room. The photo was inscribed after his reconciliation with the Church:

> To dear John and Edna,
> As a testimonial of my affectionate
> friendship. May God bless you both
> and all hope and love always.
> +Bonaventure F. Broderick
> Titular Bishop of Juliopolis, 1940[308]

Embraced by the Dutchess County Community

By December of 1935 he was in demand as a speaker and any local mystery about who he was or what his beliefs were had long evaporated. On February 13, 1936, the Poughkeepsie *Eagle-News* ran the headline "Talk Planned by Broderick, Exchange Club Hears Historic Address Tonight" followed by the announcement that "Dr. B. F. Broderick of Washington Hollow will give an historic talk tonight on 'Poughkeepsie's Proud Distinction' tonight at 6:30 o'clock at a supper meeting of the Exchange Club at the Nelson House."[309] And in another speech, his sense of humor surfaced in an uncanny forecast of our modern-day pursuit of solar energy:

> The Farm bureau members were addressed by the Rev. Dr. B. F. Broderick of Washington Hollow who emphasized the importance of balance in the "force" of the producing and consuming groups in the nation. These two groups are out of balance at present, he said, and, moreover, industry and business are out of balance themselves. Speaking on "The First Law of Nature" Dr. Broderick pointed out that forces in human relationships must, to produce satisfactory results, be in balance as are the forces of the physical and biological worlds. Striking a humorous vein, the speaker observed that if mankind thought of drawing heat, light, and power from the sun, John E. Mack, counsel of the Legislative utilities investigating committee would subject Old Sol to a stiff cross examination on his utilities business.[310]

He became known as an amateur horticulturalist and his concise history of "rebel weed" appeared in the Poughkeepsie paper.

> The magenta-purple plant in swampy land which at this season of the year makes many sections of Dutchess County a glorious riot of color is appreciated by many, although its name is known to few. Dr. B. F. Broderick who lives on the Dutchess turnpike just west of Washington Hollow has written a short history of this plant in which he states that it is not native to the mid-Hudson region but was apparently introduced first from the south through an accident, quickly naturalizing itself in the vicinity of New Paltz. The plant is commonly known as purple loosestrife but its introduction to the north occurred shortly after the Civil War and natives of

Ulster County formerly called it "rebel weed" because of its southern origins. (Poughkeepsie *News-Journal*, August 13, 1936).

Broderick's concluding paragraph of his history of the plant is worth noting as an example of his skill as a wordsmith:

> The writer of this article has beheld the poppies blooming in Flanders fields and has admired these flowers blanketing in scarlet large areas of the Roman Campagna; he has thrilled to the spectacle of the wild roses blooming in Paestum's "lovely land of doom;" he is familiar with the sight of the mountain laurel in bloom on the Litchfield hills, and of the rhodora and rhododendrons of the Catskill mountains; he has enjoyed from his childhood the beauty of meadows filled with crimson clover or with yellow-eyed daisies; and he has often been transported into an ecstasy by the exquisite hue and the delicate form of the fringed gentian growing in profusion in some soggy pasture, but never has the sight of wild flowers in any other place or under any other set of circumstances so stilled his soul with pleasure as has the spectacle of the purple loosestrife covering with its magnificence acre after acre beside the roadsides in Dutchess and Ulster counties, New York, during the second half of August each year.

J. Ogden Tyldsley, Jr. has written the present author, "I do distinctly recall that annually, in the fall, my mother would mention how (Bishop Broderick) was enamored of the purple loosestrife."

The bishop continued to travel, especially after he turned over the operation of his gas station.[311] He spent the better part of 1937 and 1938 in Irvington-on-the-Hudson, near White

Plains, New York, where David was living. In March of 1938, the Irvington Gazette reported "Bishop Broderick, who has occupied the Worthington homestead during the last year, has gone to Canada." The Worthington Homestead was the country home of Charles Campbell Worthington, heir to the "Worthington Pump" fortune garnered from his father's career of inventing, patenting, manufacturing, and selling steam pumps and waterworks engines. Popularly known as "C.C.," Charles Worthington had a private golf course on the estate, another attraction for Broderick.

How the Broderick and Worthington friendship developed is open to speculation. Worthington pumps may have been used in the Cienfuegos project, or a personal friendship may have developed through two common interests: automobiles and golf. C.C. founded the Worthington Automobile Company in 1904, later merging it with the Berg Automobile Company of Cleveland. An avid golfer, C.C. was instrumental in founding the Professional Golfers Association in 1912.[312] Broderick's interest in all things financial helped him fit in with the family: C. C.'s brother-in-law was Henry Worthington Bull, a member of the Rough Riders whose father was William Lanman Bull, one time President of the New York Stock Exchange.

The economic depression dragged on, and funds may have been running low after years of a bountiful lifestyle. He filed several lawsuits related to the rental properties he owned in the Bronx. Among the defendants were Violet Park, Inc. of the Bronx (1932), Waring Plains Cork (1933), Continental Bank & Trust Co., (1934), and Mott Haven Mortgage Corp. (1934).[313] By 1939 he had sold most of his real estate in the Bronx while he still owned one property in Manhattan. The weekly Millbrook newspaper, with its two-dollar annual subscription, would produce little revenue to a columnist, and the buying power of his $100 monthly *pensio* had diminished over thirty-four years. Whatever the circumstances, when Francis Spellman arrived on the scene the newly consecrated Archbishop of New York got the impression that Broderick was "eking out a living" with his little business—the fabled gas station that he had been trying to sell for $20,000.

10. End of Exile, 1939

As 1939 and the economic depression wore on in the United States, and while other nations continued their buildup to the Second World War, in tiny Millbrook, New York, Dr. Bonaventure Broderick continued to write his weekly column for the *Round Table* unaware that release from his long purgatory was imminent. His liberation was animated by several men, but the one who finally triggered it, in a remarkable way, was Amleto Cicognani, the middleman in the drama of the bishop's homecoming.

The Italian-born Cicognani was ordained in Italy at age 22 in 1905, the year Broderick was set adrift by Pius X. On April 23, 1933, after twenty-eight years as a priest in Faenza, Italy, he was ordained Titular Archbishop of Laodicea in Phyrgia and appointed Apostolic Delegate to the United States, a position he would hold for twenty-five years. John Tracy Ellis, historian and scholar, knew Cicognani and described him as "extraordinarily discreet" and a man who "held himself aloof from matters that did not fall within his jurisdiction."[314] It was Cicognani who brought Broderick's plight to Spellman's attention, doing so in an extraordinary way.

On the eve of Spellman's May 23 installation Cicognani met with him in the archiepiscopal residence on Madison Avenue bringing to his attention "four grave matters that needed his immediate attention. One was financial, involving an archdiocese in Peru; one legal and financial involving a college in China; one concerned a religious congregation; and one a prelate living in retirement."[315] That prelate was Broderick.

Spellman was about to become responsible for one million New York Catholics, the third largest diocese in the country and one deeply in debt.[316] The Broderick matter was decades old and forgotten by most, so why was it of such import? Why did Cicognani, a man known for his discretion, put the Broderick issue to Spellman in such urgent terms? If only four "grave matters" were to be put before him, one would think the archdiocesan debt of $28 million[317] would take precedence over a long-forgotten and aging prelate.

The Knock on the Door

Whatever the cause of Cicognani's astonishing emphasis, Spellman took the Broderick problem so seriously that he wasted little time giving it his full attention. Within four months he secretly sought him out in Dutchess County, where he found the long-exiled bishop at home on the hill above and behind his little gas station.

His visit to Washington Hollow took place early in September. It was a visit shrouded in secrecy with no publicity and no advance notice to anyone, not Broderick, not even Father Joseph Deahy, pastor of St. Joseph's in Millbrook,[318] who drove Spellman to Broderick's home. Spellman alone knew the plan. The public reason for his trip to the Millbrook area was the acceptance of a gift to the archdiocese of a private home and sixty-eight acres from Mr. Oakleigh Thorne, a wealthy Millbrook businessman.[319]

End of Exile, 1939   125

The approach to Broderick's home, the visit, and the extraordinary conversation is vividly recalled in a letter written by Spellman to Cicognani on November 27. The detail of the letter illustrates what Spellman's biographer, Robert Gannon, called the archbishop's "zeal for the preservation of the highest standards in the American hierarchy."[320] Gannon included the letter in his *The Cardinal Spellman Story*.[321]

The stirring correspondence puts the reader alongside the archbishop as he makes his way to Broderick's home, and in the room with the two prelates; one newly consecrated at age fifty, the other, a seventy-year-old who had been cast away thirty-four years earlier.

> Your Excellency:
>
> It will give Your Excellency great happiness to hear, as it gives me great consolation to recount that I have been able to bring to a satisfactory conclusion one of the problems which Your Excellency brought to my attention the night before my installation ceremonies as Archbishop. Your Excellency will remember that you told me that there was a Bishop living in the Diocese who was not living as a Bishop but instead was conducting a business establishment for the sale of automobile accessories and gasoline. Your Excellency told me that it would be a great blessing if this unfortunate individual could be reconciled with the church, for many years have elapsed since he abandoned our Holy Religion. I made a mental note of Your Excellency's story and resolved at the earliest opportunity to do what I could in this matter.
>
> I had occasion to visit Millbrook, which is a town about eighty miles from New York City, on a matter concerning the acceptance of a gift of an estate to the

Church for charitable purposes. After I had met the kind donor and inspected the property and expressed my gratitude for his gift, I excused myself from the company of priests and lay people and told the parish priest that I wanted him to drive me in his own automobile to visit a convent. I actually went to the convent, but this visitation was a pretext, as I did not care to have anyone know that my real mission was to meet the Bishop. When I was alone with the Pastor, I told him that I wanted him to take me to the home of Bishop Broderick. After arriving at the place indicated to me as the Bishop's residence, I asked the parish priest to drive on a distance, and I walked back to the house and to the door of the residence which was some considerable distance from the road. The district is not very thickly settled and there were no houses in the vicinity so my going there would be unnoticed, but I did not wish the car to be parked in front of his house in case some passing autoist might recognize it and speculate.

On my way to the house I asked the priest about the Bishop. He said that he was known as Dr. Broderick. He was respected in the community, even though it was known that the man was a Bishop of the Catholic Church. Naturally, however, his presence was, to say the least, a cause of wonderment to Catholics and non-Catholics alike.

I knocked on the door and it was opened by a man of about seventy years of age, dressed plainly in rough clothes and I took it for granted that it was the Bishop. I said, "Good afternoon, Dr. Broderick, I am Archbishop Spellman and I heard that you were here and I thought I would come to see you and ask you if there was anything I could do to help you." Immediately and spontaneously came his answer. "I have been waiting for thirty years for someone to say those words to me." I entered the house and sat down and told him that if he would like to tell me his story that I would be pleased to hear it as I knew nothing about him or the cause of his difficulties. I knew only that he was a Catholic Bishop, and I wanted to help him if I could.

He told me an interesting and moving story which I have since substantiated and have found to be the truth. He told me that he was a priest of the Diocese of Hartford, that he had studied in Rome, received his degree, returned to America, and had been appointed professor in a Seminary. Subsequently he was a pastor of an Italian parish, and had been selected by Monsignor Sbarretti, his former professor, and at that time auditor of the Apostolic Delegation in Washington, to go with him to Havana and help him in adjusting matters concerning the relations of the United States government in settlement of Church claims, and he showed me documents attesting the esteem of the highest American authorities because of his work in Cuba as Auxiliary bishop of Havana and did excellent work there. He told me that Archbishop Chapelle of New Orleans became Apostolic Delegate to Cuba, and as time went on, the Archbishop became unfriendly to him. The Archbishop went to Rome and complained about Bishop Broderick. Bishop Broderick, on his own volition, went to Rome and explained his position to the evident satisfaction of His Holiness Pius X and Cardinal Merry del Val because on the date of December 20, 1904, with document #9184 of the Secretary of State, Bishop Broderick was appointed delegate of the Holy Father to come to the United States to organize and promote in each diocese of the United States the Peter's Pence collection.

Bishop Broderick then returned to America to conduct the mission entrusted to him. When he arrived in New York he received a telegram to report to Cardinal Gibbons in Baltimore. Cardinal Gibbons treated Bishop Broderick in a somewhat abrupt manner and told him that the mission entrusted to him by the Holy See had been revoked. The Bishop was left without funds in the United States and without any work to do, and he wrote to His Holiness Pius X and informed His Holiness of his plight. The Holy Father deigned to answer Bishop Broderick in a letter written March 29, 1905, entirely in his own handwriting. Bishop Broderick showed this letter to me and permitted me to make a photostatic copy of it which I am sending to Your Excellency, and of which I have sent a copy to the Holy See by Father McCormick. Pius X explained to Bishop Broderick that he had been obliged to withdraw the authority granted to him to promote the Peter's Pence collection because of the protests that were received from many Bishops in the United States stating that this appointment of Bishop Broderick for this purpose would be interpreted as a reflection on their own capabilities and an implied reproof to the Bishops. The Holy Father then went on to say that it was not an easy thing for him to provide a diocese *immediately* to Bishop Broderick. The Holy Father referred to Bishop Broderick's plight as a small trial, indicating that at least up to that time there had been no grave charges against the Bishop. Bishop Broderick showed me many letters and he also showed me a copy of a letter which he wrote to the Holy Father saying that his situation without a place to go or to work as a Bishop would be a scandal in America. The Holy Father interpreted this observation of Bishop Broderick's as a threat to cause a scandal since the Holy Father exhorted him not to create a scandal by saying, "I do not hide from you the heavy sorrow that you have brought to my heart by your threat, in your letter, to cause a grave scandal." Bishop Broderick says he made no threat to cause a scandal. He only wanted to stress the fact that the lack of a definite assignment was in itself a scandal.

I then asked him if he would be willing to return to his duties as a priest. He told me that gladly would he do so, and the only reason that he was eking out his existence by conducting a little business was because the One Hundred ($100) Dollars pension which the Holy See had graciously granted him was not enough for him to live on.

I made inquiries of several of the Bishop's contemporaries including Cardinal (William Henry) O'Connell and Cardinal Dougherty, and also from Archbishop Murray who is from the Diocese of Hartford, and all agreed that the Bishop had not been guilty of anything wrong. There have been stories about the Bishop, but that was inevitable. Bishops, priests, and people naturally concluded that there must have been something very serious that would have brought a Bishop to such a sorry plight. It would seem that since Pius X referred to his antecedent situation as a "small trial," and since the delicate nature of a task such as Bishop Broderick had entrusted to him by the Holy See was one that could of its very nature provoked some annoyance or irritation, and since there is nothing definite of a grave charge in the files of the Apostolic Delegation concerning Bishop Broderick, and the Bishops who knew him and know him are desirous that he return to duty, and since the Bishop himself appeared to me to be very well disposed and very anxious to return to the work of the ministry and give the last few years of his life to the service of

God, for all these reasons, I appointed him chaplain of the Frances Schervier Hospital, 227th Street and Independence Avenue, Riverdale, New York, where he will have an opportunity to celebrate Mass and care for the sick and comfort them and administer the Sacraments to them. This appointment will go into effect on December 1. The Bishop desired to be a parish priest, but when I indicated to him that this would be rather difficult, at least in the beginning, he readily consented to take up this post which I offered him.

Rejoicing with Your Excellency at the happy resolution of this case which I know will have Your Excellency's approval, and with sentiments of esteem and devotion, I am

Your Excellency's devoted servant in Christ,
Francis J. Spellman
Archbishop of New York

Cicognani responded to Spellman on November 29:

It was indeed consoling to read your esteemed letter of the 27th instant, relative to the case of Bishop Broderick, and I hasten to thank you and to congratulate your Excellency for the success you have achieved in this matter. It will be a great pleasure to transmit the report to the Holy See at the first opportunity.[322]

On September 15, 1939, Broderick wrote to the archbishop:[323]

Most Reverend and Dear Archbishop:
Since it seems now that it may be ten days, or more, before I shall have given careful consideration to all the thoughts that have come into my mind in connection

with your recent much appreciated visit, and shall have prepared all the materials that I shall then wish to submit to you, to justify my asking you for an interview at which to give you definite answers to the kindly suggestions you made in my favor, I have decided not to delay longer writing you this letter for the special purpose of expressing my admiration and gratitude for the Heaven-inspired, gracious and kindly visit. Even if no further benefit were to result to me from it, I would still always regard it as the most remarkable experience of my life. Never was there brought to my attention in any way an action more Christ-like or more noble. Every detail and incident of it, every word and look we exchanged shall always remain impressed on my memory as long as I live. You have done much to restore my badly shaken confidence in human nature. Fortunately, I have never permitted bitterness to lodge in my soul. Divine grace has never allowed my faith in God to be weakened. Through all the years of my misery, my constant and fervent prayer has been: "God is Good." I like to believe that it was in answer to that prayer that He inspired you to visit me and speak to me in the way you did last Tuesday.

Again, thanking you for your great goodness to me, and praying God to bless you always, I have the honor to be

    Very Sincerely and gratefully yours in Christ,
        Bonaventure F. Broderick
          Tit. Bishop of Juliopolis

Spellman's Due Diligence Addressed the Question of Helen Bowlen

Spellman, in addition to having a full understanding of Broderick's ecclesiastical troubles was aware of the 1912 investigation by Cardinal Farley, his predecessor twice removed, into the person of Helen Bowlen. Spellman requested a personal interview, and she wrote him[324] from Dutchess County on December 1, 1939:

> Dear Archbishop Spellman,
> I am writing this note to comply with the indications contained in the message recently sent me by you through Bishop Broderick that I send you my N.Y. City address and that I write you to arrange an appointment for a personal interview.
> In the present my N.Y. City address will be 3169 Hull Ave., and I shall find it most convenient to keep any appointment you may wish to make for me.
> Thanking you for your great kindness, I have the honor to be most respectfully,
>
> (signed) Helen M. Bowlen

Satisfied with the interview, he accelerated the restoration of the long-exiled and aging prelate. John Deedy, in *Seven American Catholics*, summed it best: "Spellman's was a compassionate action correcting an injustice that had resulted largely from misunderstanding."[325]

Saintly Patience Wins the Day

In June of 1962 syndicated columnist Jim Bishop reviewed Gannon's biography. The columnist singled out the Broderick story as one of the great anecdotes Gannon shares in the 400-

plus page biography, noting that Spellman was under no obligation to do what he did.[326]

The lack of obligation aside, what is fascinating is that Cicognani not only brought Broderick's plight to Spellman's attention, but did so on the eve of his consecration, making it a top priority for the new archbishop.

The question remains: after several decades of estrangement, why the sudden interest in the Broderick difficulty? It was not so sudden. John Cooney, in *The American Pope* writes "Why the Vatican decided to do so at this late date is open to speculation. The Romans responsible for his punishment may simply have died off or forgiven him."[327] It is true that the early antagonists were deceased: Chapelle (1905), Redding (1911), Pius X (1914), Gibbons (1921) and Merry de Val (1930). They were gone but one of his key supporters and the cleric who knew best Broderick's whole history, the Italian Donato Sbarretti, was living and well-placed in Rome.

Sbarretti was Broderick's professor in Rome in the late 1890s and when elevated to Bishop of Havana in 1900 removed the then-young priest from his uncomfortable situation with Bishop Tierney in Connecticut, taking him to Cuba as his secretary, where the two were publicly commended for their work in settling the Church property question. As a result, Broderick was made a monsignor in 1901 and Auxiliary Bishop of Havana in 1903. While Broderick was exiled, Sbarretti continued his climb, first as apostolic delegate to Canada and Newfoundland, then Secretary of the Congregation of the Affairs of Religious, elevated to Cardinal in 1916, then Prefect of the Congregation of the Council, and finally in 1930, Secretary of the Congregation of the Holy Office, replacing the late Cardinal Merry de Val. By 1930 he had been in Rome fourteen years.

Three years later, in 1933, the fifty-year-old Cicognani was appointed apostolic delegate to the United States. Sbarretti had the ear of his fellow Italian. Gerald Fogarty, in *Patterns of Episcopal Leadership*, writes that it was in 1933 that Cicognani was told to work on Broderick's restoration.[328] Who told Cicognani? Likely it was Sbarretti; he was in the perfect position to tell the apostolic delegate of his old friend's plight.

This begs the question: If Cicognani was told in 1933 to work on Broderick's restoration, why did it take six years to unfold?

Cicognani may have tried to intercede on behalf of Broderick with Spellman's predecessor, Cardinal Patrick Hayes, as early as 1933, but Hayes had earlier served as auxiliary bishop, beginning in 1914, to Cardinal Farley, a close associate of Gibbons, and may have been infected with the same antagonism toward Broderick as Gibbons. Additionally, Hayes had been Chancellor of the archdiocese in 1912 and was the one who prepared and forwarded to Cardinal Merry del Val a summary of the investigation into the alleged marriage of Broderick. The passing of the torch to Spellman after Hayes' death in 1938 was the opening for Cicognani to move aggressively on Sbarretti's request.

Sbarretti did not live to see the reconciliation; he died in Rome at age 82 on April 1, 1939, two weeks before Spellman was appointed archbishop.

Another Broderick supporter who had Cicognani's ear was John G. Murray, Archbishop of Saint Paul, Minnesota. Like Broderick, Murray was a priest of the Hartford Diocese, ordained in 1900, the year the Broderick Projectile Company went bankrupt. If Sbarretti sparked the first request of Cicognani in 1933 it was Murray who turned up the heat early in 1939.

In 1938 Murray wrote to Monsignor F. Keegan, then Executive Director of Catholic Charities of New York, asking about Broderick's status. Keegan left no stone unturned. In addition to contacting Monsignor Stephen Connelly, the Dean of Clergy in Dutchess County, he hired a private investigator. In January of 1939, he sent his findings to Murray. "He has a farm on Washington Hollow on the road to Millbrook. I went there some years ago and he had a gas station which he has since given over to someone else. He dresses in a khaki outfit and mingles with the people both in Millbrook and Pleasant Valley, to whom he is known as 'Doctor.' He has given no reason for criticism or scandal."[329]

The private investigator added little of note. "His property has been for sale for some time and he once had an asking price of $20,000. He has a 1937 Chevrolet automobile. Prior to that he had an old 1928 car. He is evidently well-known in the vicinity and is referred to as both 'Bishop' and 'Doctor.' He does not enjoy good health and is under the care of a Doctor White in Millbrook."[330]

Murray replied to Keegan on January 11, 1939, telling him,

> My interest in the subject of the investigation was due to the fact that his great friend and counsel in all his legal problems, Mr. William Brosmith, Vice-President of the Travelers Insurance Company and Trustee of the Hartford Cathedral for the past thirty-five years, died a year ago. I met the Bishop at the funeral of Mrs. Brosmith twenty years ago. Now that his friend is dead and no one else interested apparently, I felt impelled to approach

with an offer of aid of some kind if the step could be taken with propriety. Under the circumstances you have been of great help in my reaching the decision to make known my attitude.[331]

Cicognani, as the Apostolic Delegate to the United States, would be the person for Murray to make known his attitude.

Spellman sent Murray a copy of his November 27 letter to Cicognani, the letter that captured his visit to Broderick. Murray responded to Spellman on December 22, 1939. "The enclosed letter is certainly worth all the trouble you had in trying to adjust what in my opinion was a major problem in the Church of the U.S.A. God bless you for your charity, zeal, and decision in this as in your many other activities."[332]

Another old friend who may have influenced Cicognani's decision to move on the Broderick problem was Bishop Joseph P. Lynch of the Diocese of Dallas, a classmate of Broderick's at St. Charles College in Emmitsburg. A third classmate, Chris C. Keenan, longtime Supreme President of the Catholic Benevolent League in New York City wrote to Lynch only days after Cardinal Hayes death in 1938 about "the titular Bishop of Juliopolis whom you and I knew when we were all much younger than we are now, as Boni Broderick, but now living as a retired country gentleman on a seventy-acre estate in the fastnesses of Dutchess Co., New York and known generally as Dr. Broderick ... I am going to give you a thumb nail sketch of what I know about him."

> In the first place I found him to be the same genial, gentle, and generous soul we knew in the old days. In the second place, I found that many stories currently being

told about him were just not true. I know very little about his history during all these years. He became a bishop in 1903. I have made no effort to embarrass him by ferreting into his history. I know nothing whatever about his present status. He has volunteered some information such for instance as that he is in receipt from Rome at regular intervals of a stipend or honorarium and that he has never been reprimanded or disciplined by anyone in authority.

My belief is he has become the victim of Church politics. I can't know whether his status is such as to make hopeless any attempt to get him straightened out.

However, that may be, I have grown very fond of him and no matter what has happened to leave him high and dry as he is, I feel he has been more sinned against than sinning.[333]

Accolades for Spellman's Action

Spellman sent a copy of his November 27 letter to his old friend, Richard Cushing, then the recently consecrated Auxiliary Bishop of Boston. Cushing replied on December 15, 1939:

I am returning the letter in re: Dr. Broderick. What a beautiful act of charity you performed. I never read anything that made such a profound impression on me. As I frequently said—The Hand of the Lord is upon you. To me you have started a new era in the hierarchy of this country. An era of heart that will bring souls nearer to their spiritual leaders. May God give you the strength to carry on.[334]

Noted theologian, author and lecturer Father Owen B. McGuire, then of Elmira, New York, wrote to Spellman on September 28, 1940:

> I want to take the opportunity to congratulate and thank you for the restoration of Bishop Broderick. I learned of it first last May when I had gone down to the Golden Jubilee of my old friend Denis Dougherty (Denis and I were contemporaries at the Roman College for four years). On my way back via New York I called up the Bishop one night and went to see him the next day. The only baggage I had with me was a walking stick (to help a broken leg) but he had a room prepared for me for the night. It was one of the happiest days of my life.
>
> The reason why his restoration brought me such joy is that I had for some years sought opportunity to try my own hand in solving the problem, but the opportunity never came, and I must say that I found little sympathy among those when I approached and who had known him at the Collegio. Usually their advice was "Have nothing to do with him." Very different was the response of Cardinal Sbarretti when I called on him in Rome two years ago.
>
> Bonny Broderick, as we called him, came to the college after I left for Innsbruck when I made the course in theology. But for reasons it is not necessary to mention, I was 'the talk of the college' for some time after I left. So, he knew of me. When my health broke and after a second operation on the stomach, I was staying at my sisters in New York. The Bishop was then living in Yonkers. I don't know how he got my address, but he came to see me and comfort me, and as I was badly in need of comfort and encouragement, I could never forget his kind thoughtfulness on that occasion. He had a kind heart

and a love for the poor and suffering. And he did a work under Sbarretti in Cuba that, I believe, could not have been done by any other man available at the time. May God reward you for his restoration.[335]

Broderick Prepares to Move

John O. Tyldsley, publisher and editor of the *Millbrook Round Table* bade his columnist farewell in an editorial on November 3, 1939:

> Reluctantly has the *Round Table* submitted to the dictum that Dr. Broderick should curtail the regularity of his contributions to its columns ... we do not feel, however that we can allow our distinguished co-worker to leave our staff without further comment. His work with us has been of too high a caliber to admit of silence. In his weekly column ... Dr. Broderick bespoke his mind and heart with singular freedom. From his writings one could gain information. But the regular reader gained much more—a glimpse into the life and thought of a deeply religious personality.
>
> Over the course of many years Dr. Broderick has rendered services to his fellow men in many parts of the world. But to us in Millbrook there will always be the more lively memory of a work directed at this small community. We have gained much from his fruitful thinking, which bears the mark of a long and varied and successful career. He brought to his work as editor and columnist a mellowness which is rare and a point of view flavored with experience and tolerance.

Broderick clipped the above editorial and sent it to Spellman on November 14, 1939, with a note reading "This is just a sentence or two to say that I am making satisfactory progress with my preparations, and that I shall report for duty as you so kindly arranged at our last interview. I thought you might be interested in seeing the enclosed clipping from the Millbrook Round Table."[336]

11. Reconciled Years, 1940-1943

Frances Schervier Hospital and Home

Effective December 1, 1939, Most Reverend Bonaventure Broderick[337] was appointed chaplain of the Frances Schervier Hospital and Home. The hospital, named after the foundress of the Sisters of the Poor of Saint Francis religious order, was nestled on seven acres overlooking the Hudson in the Riverdale neighborhood of the Bronx. He made haste to the newly built facility where he assumed residence and where he also ministered to the forty Franciscan sisters staffing the facility.

Within a week of his arrival, he wrote a note of gratitude to Spellman:[338]

> I arrived at this little heaven last Saturday afternoon, and was enchanted with it from the very start, and am each day, becoming more strongly confirmed in my first impressions. The sisters here are certainly doing God's work in an exemplary fashion. My health is improving notably, I am getting accustomed to the routine of my duties rapidly, and I am very happy. I thank Your Excellency and am praying to God to bless Your Excellency for all your kindness to me.

The excitement of his return to active ministry was soon tempered by the death of his brother. David died on January 2, 1940, at age 73. He had suffered a lingering illness in White Plains, New York, where he had been living for many years. His obituary recalled, without criticism, the earlier days when "during the Spanish-American War Mr. Broderick, with his brother, Clement M. Broderick, operated a projectile fuse plant in Windsor. His brother died shortly after the Spanish-American War and Mr. Broderick later became connected with various plants in and near Hartford. He spent several years as a young man in Cuba helping construct one of the largest water systems in the world at that time."[339]

Rome Delays

An unexpected, but short-lived, setback in the full rehabilitation of Bishop Broderick occurred almost immediately; one that Broderick was likely unaware of and perhaps never learned of. Cicognani outlined the problem in a letter to Spellman dated January 25, 1940, and cloaked in anonymity:

> In a recent communication you expressed regrets that the case of a certain gentleman in whom we have both been interested could not be treated by the Secretariate of State and the Sacred Consistorial Congregation ... and I was myself quite surprised some weeks ago to receive an interrogation regarding him from the Holy Office. In writing me, His Eminence, Cardinal Marchetti, offered no reason for the interest of the Holy Office in the case except to mention certain documents dating back to 1913; but he ordered me to give a full report on the case as it might appear from the Delegation files. I incorporated into my report the recent efforts made on behalf of

the man in question, setting in relief both your own and my favorable viewpoints. I trust sincerely that the report will be accepted, and that we shall hear no more in the matter.[340]

Marchetti had succeeded Donato Sbarretti as Secretary of the Holy Office, named to that position by Pius XII after Sbarretti's death nine months earlier. The obstacle was likely the investigation of the "marriage" rumor; an inquiry begun in 1912 by Monsignor Cerretti in the office of the Apostolic Delegation and conducted by then-Archbishop Farley and others.

True to Cicognani's prediction, the Holy Office promptly completed its investigation[341] of Broderick, allowing for his full restoration to episcopal ministry. In February, Spellman decided it was time for the long-exiled bishop to appear in procession wearing the robes of his rank, and the ceremony for conferring the pallium took place in St. Patrick's Cathedral.

The Gas Station is Sold

After Helen Bowlen moved to Hull Street in Brooklyn, she sold the property in Washington Hollow, though the inclusion of a gas station seemed an afterthought to the sale. The Poughkeepsie paper reported the sale and noted the property consisted of several barns and other outbuildings, had recently been remodeled with alterations that included installation of a large swimming pool, and that "there is also a small gas station."[342]

The Sisters of the Poor of St. Francis

Bishop Broderick was well received at Schervier. The Sisters of the Poor of St. Francis, whose American foundation was set up in 1868, numbered 2,500 religious in the United States in

1940. The sisters were active in New York hospital ministry from the first day of their founding; in Brooklyn, at St. Peter's Hospital and St. Anthony Hospital, and in the Bronx at St. Joseph Hospital and St. Francis.[343] To these was added the Frances Schervier Hospital, constructed in 1937.[344]

Reading the text of the speech delivered by Father Peter Duffee at the laying of the cornerstone in 1938 one recognizes Spellman's genius in assigning Broderick, long-hungering for a return to the Lord's vineyard, to the 410-bed nursing facility:

> This home for the chronically ill is the antithesis of modern political and economic systems that have degraded humanity to the baseness of cheapness. In the modern age, when a highly mechanized world looks with pity upon those who have worn out the limited capacities of human nature and esteems them to be useless members of society and a drag on economic progress, this charitable hospital, constructed by and because of the charity of Christ, will accord them their proper place of honor and pity in the divine scheme of the universe.[345]

In 1989, seminarian Thomas Ginty interviewed several of the Franciscan sisters who knew their chaplain well. Among their many memories was how he ably served as "a trusted advisor" to Mother Maria, the superior, "concerning such matters as overcoming the zoning commission's refusal to allow a new convent to be completed and helping her raise the funds needed to pay the mortgage and eventually expand the facility."[346]

They also shared memories of his kindness. Shortly after Broderick's arrival one of the sisters, unaware that the bishop was in the room, complained that her shoes were too small, and they were causing her great discomfort. She soon had new shoes.

On another occasion he bought the sisters fishing rods. They remembered him as "content in his new position" and "willing to help in any way he could."[347]

One sister recalled that when he spoke about his time in Cuba, "he would literally cry like a baby." This sadness, she offered, was "due to the way he had been treated by the bishops in Cuba," and that "they were jealous of him because of his popularity with the people."[348]

Writer, Author, Correspondent

The same sister added that he freely spoke about his years in the Millbrook area and "was proud of his writing ability which had been reflected in his published works."[349]

Among Broderick's works were three self-published texts recounting some of his archaeological achievements. One was published in 1940: the thirty-nine page *The So-Called Altar of Calvinus on the Platine Hill, in Rome; Identified as the Altar Erected by Romulus as a Part of the Ceremony of Founding Rome.*

This was followed by a second, longer, illustrated edition in 1941 retitled *The Forum Stele, in the Lapis Niger at Rome, Identified as the Sole Recognizable Remnant of the Wreck of the Original Altar Erected by Romulus as a Part of his Ceremony of Formally Founding the City of Rome and its Inscription Interpreted.*

The third book, also published in 1941, though copyrighted in 1931, was titled the *Lapis Niger*[350] *in the Comitium at Rome, Identified as the Traditional Tomb of Romulus, and its Identity, its History, and its Importance Discussed.*

In the brief volumes he recalled his expeditions of the late 1890s while noting that he revisited the digs in 1901 (at the time of his private audience with Leo XIII) and again in 1904 (while he was in Rome to defend himself against the charges made by Archbishop Chapelle).

In his Introduction to *The So-Called Altar of Calvinus* (1940) he wrote:

> As a young man I spent nearly seven years in Rome and its environs, and during this period, under the direction of Professors Armellini and Marucchi, devoted much time to a careful study of the ruins and monuments of ancient Rome and of the sacred and historical places of that most interesting of all cities. In the course of my work with these and other distinguished scholars I had the honor of meeting the great Mommsen, the celebrated De Rossi, and the illustrious Duchesne, and of being treated with friendly appreciation by all of these.[351]

In the summer of 1940 news broke that Pope Pius XII, after traces of a fourth century church were found in work under the sixteenth-century basilica named after Saint Peter, authorized the archaeological dig in search of Peter's original tomb. Broderick received a letter from attorney-friend Thomas H. Baskerville of the firm of Middlebrook & Sincerbeaux who enclosed a newspaper clipping with an Associated Press report on the event. The column was titled "Vatican Seeks First Grave of Apostle Peter." The column was accompanied by a note recalling Broderick's pioneering success as a graffitologist: "Dear Bishop, please read the enclosed clipping. It shows that what you started forty years ago has now been adopted but the Pope will probably take all the credit, and you, the original discoverer, will be forgotten."[352]

In the two books published in 1941, he wrote: "Grateful acknowledgement is made, and my sincere thanks is offered to my dear friend, Raoul E. Desvernine, Esq. of New York City for the kind encouragement and great help he has given me in the preparation and publication of this monograph."

His friendship with Desvernine underscores Broderick's extensive networking among those with connections to Cuba. A native New Yorker of Cuban descent, Desvernine had careers in both law and industry. In 1909 he was Counsel to the Cuban legation in Washington, D.C., and later president of Crucible Steel Company. Like Broderick, he was a foe of Franklin Roosevelt's social policies and was at one time chair of the American Liberty League, an anti-New Deal organization formed in 1934.[353] His 1936 book, *Democratic Despotism*, was published by Dodd, Mead & Co. In 1935 he cofounded the Catholic Thought Association with, among others, Thomas Woodlock, editor of the *Wall Street Journal* and future author of *The Catholic Pattern* (Simon and Schuster, 1943). The first object of the Manhattan-based association affiliated with the Order of Preachers (Dominicans) was "to promote among our own people a wider knowledge, appreciation and understanding of the Thomistic philosophy both in itself and in its application to the problems of the day."[354] Raoul received many honors for his services to the Church, including the designation of Knight Commander of the Holy Sepulchre with Star.[355] He died in 1966 at the age of seventy-four.

But it was Raoul's uncle, Pablo Desvernine, who enjoyed Broderick's longest and deepest friendship. The bishop kept a scrapbook[356] wherein he collected correspondence from diplomats including Mark Hanna of Ohio, General Leonard Wood, Elihu Root and others. The largest number of letters retained, covering several decades, are those from Pablo Desvernine

(1852-1935), lawyer, professor, orator, and diplomat. Desvernine was the Minister of Finance immediately following the Spanish-American War and later served as Cuba's Secretary of State, and Minister to the United States.

In a letter dated January 4, 1926, Pablo wrote to Broderick from Havana gently chastising the bishop's scrawled handwriting while lamenting the distance between them:

> You cannot have a measure of my extreme happiness at receiving your good letter of the 20th of last month instead of the customary, rigid greeting card usual in this season. I would have answered it immediately, but I had no typewriter to do it for me who, as you know, has forgotten the art of penmanship. I have my idea that you also do somewhat suffer of this imperfection for which reason I am glad, that, this time, you used the typewriting machine, relieving me of the painful task of making out your hieroglyphics which sometimes only a Champollion could interpret. You are right when you say it's a pity that, being as we are so close friends, we should not come together more often.

Pablo Desvernine died in Cuba on December 20, 1935. His obituary, dateline Havana, in the *Chicago Tribune* was brief: "Prof. Pablo Desvernine, 81, president of the State Council of Law, died last night of uremia. In his active life Professor Desvernine was graduated from Columbia University, became a member of the Revolutionary Junta In New York, was made Minister to Washington and then served as Secretary of the Treasury under Governor General John R. Brooke during the United States occupation following the Spanish-American War." Had Broderick written the obituary it would have been much more detailed. He was aware of his friend's declining health three years earlier when, with his command of language on full display, he wrote his friend,

> It is difficult for me to picture you to myself as old and sorrowing. On the contrary, I love to think of you as the keen vivacious friend whose wit and wisdom and kindliness made our companionship of years so delightful, and renders the memories of our friendship so precious to me: as the profound scholar and masterful teacher, who for a generation or more surrounded himself with a great school of loving disciples, and at whose feet I have always considered it a privilege and an honor to have sat figuratively and informally; as a sprightly gentleman of a deep and varied culture, who had enriched his mind and adorned his manners with the priceless spoils of his well-ordered excursions deeply into nearly every department of polite learning—language, literature, mathematics, history, philosophy, law, music, painting, sculpture—as the leading lawyer of his land, towering both in theory and in practice—in the written as well as in the spoken word—like a giant above even the tallest of his fellows; as a diplomat, who represented his country in its most important legation, at a most trying time, with great benefit to his fatherland and with much honor to himself; as a prudent and courageous statesman, who guided the ship of state of the newly-founded republic that governed his native island, for many years successfully through a very troubled period of its history and of the history of the world; as a loving husband and a fond father, who was the head of a household that it was a joy for anybody to enter, and in which I always felt as much at home as beside my own fireside.[357]

It may have been Pablo who introduced Helen Bowlen and Broderick. He is the only correspondent discovered whose letters reference her, always asking the bishop to give his regards to Helen, and in one, he refers to her as "Helena." When Helen first went to Havana in 1900 as Sr. Mary of St. Helena, Desvernine was the Minister of Finance, and the government was the funding agent for the reform school for girls where she was assigned. His familiarity with Helen makes it likely that he had a hand in the decision she made in 1901 to leave the congregation to care for Margaret Broderick.

Travels with the Archbishop

For the next few years, in Robert Gannon's words, "the Titular Bishop of Juliopolis was a familiar figure in the cathedral and at religious functions throughout the archdiocese, winning hearts everywhere with his simplicity, humility and gracious courtly manner."[358] The day after St. Patrick's Day 1941 New York's *Daily News* carried a front-page photo of Spellman flanked by a smiling Broderick and Bishop Stephen J. Donahue as they viewed the parade.[359] Often appearing alongside Spellman, Broderick, aware that he towered over the much shorter archbishop, would, when possible, stand on a lower step.

One appearance early in 1940 must have been particularly gratifying. With Spellman, he returned to Connecticut for the consecration of Henry Joseph O'Brien as Auxiliary Bishop of Hartford.[360]

A sampling of other events where the two were together includes the laying of the cornerstone for a new high school, Cardinal Hayes Memorial High School;[361] commencement at the College at Mount St. Vincent;[362] the St. Vincent Hospital

School of Nursing Golden Jubilee; the Red Mass presided by Spellman in Manhattan; Requiem Mass in St. Patrick's Cathedral for Mother Marie Vincentia, the superior general for the Sisters of Charity of St. Vincent de Paul;[363] observance in the Monastery of the Visitation in Riverdale marking the tercentenary of the death of St. Frances de Chantal, foundress of the Visitation order;[364] at the Hotel Astor for the 450th anniversary of the landing of Columbus with the Knights of Columbus;[365] at Catholic Verein and National Catholic Women's Union with Spellman presiding.

On June 6, 1941, Broderick was in the sanctuary of St. Patrick's Cathedral when Archbishop Spellman addressed 3,000 persons attending a Pontifical Mass for the suffering people of Great Britain.[366] And in September of the same year, in what must have been a delightful day for Broderick, he was with Spellman when Amleto Cicognani, his Roman intercessor, was given an honorary degree from Fordham University by then university president Father Robert Gannon, future biographer of Spellman.[367] Later that year, he and Spellman were two of 102 bishops who attended the Annual meeting of the Archbishops and Bishops of the United States held at Catholic University of America in Washington, D.C.[368]

Vicar for Religious

Spellman appointed Bishop Broderick Vicar of Religious for the Archdiocese, effective March 26, 1942, an assignment he held until his death and where "he cultivated a knowledge of the communities of Sisters and of Brothers in the Archdiocese and gave to them the benefit of his long and rich experience."[369]

That same month, Spellman paid a tremendous compliment to Broderick during the dedication of a new wing of the Schervier facility. During his talk, with the chaplain in the room, the archbishop uttered these words that betray the emotions and feelings that their friendship evoked: "The greatest thing I have done for my soul and the greatest gift I have brought to the people of the archdiocese has been in bringing Bishop Broderick to New York."[370]

Broderick's activity as Vicar of Religious included such duties as presiding at a Mass in the Bronx for eight Carmelite nuns professing final vows [371] and at the Capuchin Monastery of the Sacred Heart Youth Day and Flag Day Solemn Mass, at which the Yonkers *Herald Statesman* reported the bishop "told the boys and girls that self-respect is one of the most important human attributes."[372] And he represented Archbishop Spellman at liturgies such as the funeral Mass in Manhattan for Mother Mary Rosarie, the Mother Superior of the Sisters of the Reparation of the Congregation of Mary[373] and the Solemn Novena of Reparation at St. Leo's in Manhattan.[374]

In December of 1942 he and Spellman presided at the departure ceremony for seventeen Maryknoll missionaries headed to Bolivia.[375]

One of his last official functions was the blessing of the Reliquary of the North American Martyrs in the university chapel at Fordham University.[376]

Little correspondence remains from his restored years but the December before he died he wrote to Cardinal Denis Dougherty, who was three years his elder and Archbishop of Philadelphia. Dougherty was one of the men in 1939 who provided Spellman with favorable feedback on Broderick's character. Reminding Dougherty that they both were consecrated bishops in 1903 and together thrown into the aftermath of the Spanish American War, Broderick wrote:

> Recalling the similarities of our experiences—yours in the Philippines and mine in Cuba—I write you this little note to send you my greetings for a Merry Christmas, a Happy New Year, and a Joyous Holy Season. May Peace be yours on Earth, Glory in Heaven, and God's choicest Blessings everywhere![377]

The similarities of experience? They both had to deal the same Apostolic Delegate, Broderick's nemesis, Archbishop Chapelle.

Death Draws Near

Broderick's health, always a question mark, was in decline when Spellman reconciled him, betraying the brilliance of Spellman's decision to assign him to the Schervier Hospital and Home where his care was assured while he ministered to others. With his singular life of both worldly achievement and ministry to the sick and dying, Broderick would have appreciated the words of Flannery O'Connor: "Sickness before death is a very appropriate thing and I think those who don't have it miss one of God's mercies. Success is almost as isolating, and nothing points out vanity as well."[378]

He began to worry about Helen Bowlen, whose health was also failing. Recalling both the reason Helen came into the household in 1901 and his promise at his mother's deathbed in 1917, in his unstable hand he scribbled in a notebook what appears to be a November 1941 draft of a letter destined for the Mother Superior of the Sisters of the Poor of Saint Francis:

> Forty years ago today Miss Helen Bowlen came to live at Yonkers, N.Y. with my dearly beloved mother, who was then in her seventy second year. I had recently been selected as the Secretary of the Apostolic Delegate to the Philippine Islands and was then in the United States arranging for meeting between the President of the United States, Secretary of State John Hay, and the Secretary of War, Elihu Root, and the Most Rev. Donato Sbaretti, Archbishop of Ephesus,[379] the newly appointed Apostolic Delegate to the Philippines.[380]
>
> Now Miss Bowlen is sixty-five years old and is quite seriously sick. For the past two years I have been seriously preoccupied with the thought of providing (illegible) best possible care and comfort for Miss Bowlen.

He wrote of his desire to have Helen cared for in the Frances Schervier Home "after my death or the permanent discontinuance of my connection with this institution by any other means." He intended to enclose a check and wrote, "please find a cheque in the amount of Four Thousand Dollars drawn under date of November 3, 1941, to the order of the Frances Schervier Hospital, on the Bank of Millbrook, N.Y. by Helen M. Bowlen."

He noted it was the first payment on the sum of $7,500.00 for the life care of Miss Bowlen "in a two-window room with bath in the Friedsam Foundation Wing of the Frances Schervier Hospital in accordance with the plans and arrangements you and I discussed in our several conversations on the subject of providing in the best possible way for Miss Bowlen's care and comfort.

These matters I have fully discussed with Miss Bowlen and have duly obtained her consent to arrange with you for this care."[381]

Helen outlived Bonaventure by six years and when she died in 1949, she was in the care of the sisters at the Schervier Hospital and Home. In 1945, two years after Bonaventure's death, she purchased a plot in Gate of Heaven Cemetery where her mortal remains are interred in a section neighboring his.

Bishop Broderick lived at the Schervier facility, "this little heaven" as he called it, until his death, with Francis Spellman at his side, at half-past two o'clock the morning of Thursday, November 18, 1943, five weeks shy of his seventy-fifth birthday. The cause of death was coronary thrombosis, hypertensive cardio-vascular disease, generalized arterio-sclerosis.[382]

Spellman's Comforting Presence

Author Brendan Finn was in the process of drafting his book *Twenty-Four American Cardinals* (Bruce Publishing, 1947) when Broderick died. He attended the funeral and committal rites at the cemetery in Hawthorne, where the bishop's remains are buried in the Franciscan Sisters plot. Following the obsequies, he was compelled to write to Spellman.

> As a devoted admirer of Bishop Broderick, I was especially grateful for what Your Excellency said at the cemetery and for the way you said it. Your path is far removed from mine, but I think I know something of the way you felt about the bishop deep down in your heart. You see, I too loved him and had come to appreciate his example of patience and charity, his cheerfulness in spite of his impaired health and his devotion to the sick and dying, and to his work as vicar for religious.

> The bishop was most kind to me and I shall always treasure the many delightful hours I spent in his company at various times during these past two years. Each time I went to interview him he did everything possible to make me feel at ease and to help me. He was one of the most courteous and thoughtful men I ever knew. He had a marvelous memory and from it he could draw the most delightful stories and such a procession of facts, places, dates, etc., as would fascinate anyone.
>
> He was very devoted to you and never tired of telling me of your kindness to him. He missed you keenly while you were abroad. He would often tell me "The Archbishop is so good to me! He is always afraid I am not happy here and continually asks me if there is anything he can do for me."

Finn closed his letter with gratitude that Spellman was at Broderick's bedside as death approached:

> I know how much Your Excellency meant to him and I am so glad that Almighty God granted him the comfort of your presence as the end drew near. [383]

No doubt that was a consoling moment, but the comfort of Spellman's presence truly began four years earlier when, with the Hand of the Lord upon him, he climbed the narrow path to call on Bishop Broderick at his home nestled on a hillside behind a little two-pump gas station.

The archbishop presided at the funeral Mass in St. Patrick's Cathedral, assisted by Father Robert Gannon. Fifty-one *monsignori* assisted in the sanctuary and 150 of Bishop Broderick's beloved Franciscan Sisters of the Poor attended. Auxiliary

Bishop Francis McIntyre delivered the eulogy, finishing his tribute with a commanding summary:

> Young Bonaventure Broderick was blessed by God with an abundance of qualities for the great distinction he acquired and for the very special and diplomatic services he rendered the Church, particularly during the years he spent in the Diocese of Havana, Cuba. Talented in mind, gifted in languages, studious in disposition, able in administration, he combined in his priestly and episcopal character the attributes of a true follower of Christ who answered the call "Come, follow me."[384]

Bibliography

Bucher, Arline and Tehan, John, *Prince of Democracy, Prince of Democracy: James Cardinal Gibbons*. Garden City, NY: Hanover House, 1962.

Cooney, John, *The American Pope: The Life and Times of Francis Cardinal Spellman*. New York; Times Books, 1984.

Deedy, John, *Seven American Catholics*. Chicago: The Thomas More Press, 1978.

Ellis, John Tracy, *Catholic Bishops: A Memoir*. Wilmington, Delaware: Michael Glazier, Inc., 1983.

Finn, Brendan A., *Twenty-Four American Cardinals*, Boston: Bruce Humphries, Inc., 1947.

Fogarty, S.J., Gerald P., ed., *Patterns of Episcopal Leadership*. New York: Macmillan Publishing Company, 1989.

_____, *The Vatican and the American Hierarchy from 1870 to 1965*. Wilmington, Delaware: Michael Glazier, Inc., 1985.

Gannon, S.J., Robert I., *The Cardinal Spellman Story*. Garden City, NY: Doubleday & Company, Inc., 1962.

Ginty, Thomas M., 1989. Bonaventure Finnbar Broderick 1868-1943. Master's thesis, Mount St. Mary's Seminary.

Ginty, Msgr. Thomas M. and Medina, Miss Maria, eds., *Lift High the Cross: The History of the Archdiocese of Hartford*. Strasbourg: Editions du Signe, 2003.

Gollin, James, *Worldly Goods*. New York: Random House, 1971.

Groeschel, C.F.R., Benedict J., *Arise from Darkness*. San Francisco: Ignatius Press, 1995.

Hennesey, S.J., James, *American Catholics: A History of the Roman Catholic Community in the United States*. Oxford: Oxford University Press, 1981.

Hertz, Solange, *The Star-Spangled Heresy: Americanism*, Santa Monica: Veritas Press, 1992.

O'Toole, George J. A., *The Spanish War: An American Epic 1898*. New York: W. W. Norton & Company, 1984.

Reuter, Frank T., *Catholic Influence on American Colonial Polices 1898-1904*. Austin: University of Texas Press, 1967.

Reynolds, Kelly, *Henry Plant: Pioneer Empire Builder*. Cocoa, Florida: The Florida Historical Society Press, 2010.

Ricca, Brad, *Mrs. Sherlock Holmes*, New York: St. Martin's Press, 2016.

Risen, Clay, *The Crowded Hour: Theodore Roosevelt, the Rough Riders, and the Dawn of the American Century*. New York: Scribner, 2019.

Notes

[1] Handwritten note, Sisters of the Good Shepherd Archives, St. Louis.

[2] Robert I. Gannon, S.J., *The Cardinal Spellman Story* (Garden City, New York: Doubleday & Company, 1962), 146. (Letter from Francis Spellman to Amleto Cicognani, dated November 27, 1939).

[3] "Sbarretti's Secretary," *Hartford Courant*, December 26, 1901, 9.

[4] "Spellman Opens New Hospital Unit," *New York Times*, March 16, 1942, 32.

[5] Bridgette A. Woodall, Archdiocesan Archivist, Roman Catholic Archdiocese of Hartford, CT, letter to author dated December 15, 2021.

[6] Gannon, "Spellman," 146.

[7] Ibid., (Letter from Francis Spellman to Amleto Cicognani, dated November 27, 1939).

[8] November 19, 1910, Broderick registered a "Stanley" automobile (Kingston *Daily Freeman*).

[9] James Hennesey, S.J., *American Catholics, A History of the Roman Catholic Community in the United States* (New York: Oxford University Press, 1981).

[10] Ibid. 219.

[11] Gerald P. Fogarty, ed., *Patterns of Episcopal Leadership* (New York: Macmillan Publishing Co., 1989).

[12] Ibid. 124.

[13] Gannon, "Spellman."

[14] Benedict J. Groeschel, C.F.R., *Arise from Darkness* (San Francisco: Ignatius Press, 1995), 68-70.

[15] A patent for such a device, applied for in 1939, is attributed to a Richard Corson, then of Olean, NY. US Patent No. 231694.

[16] Thomas M. Ginty, "Bonaventure Finnbarr Broderick," M.A. thesis, Mount St. Mary's Seminary, Emmitsburg, MD, 1989.

[17] "Havana's Triple Consecration," *Boston Globe*, Boston, MA, October 28, 1903, 7.

[18] Gergely Baics, *"The Saloons of Hartford's East Side 1870-1920"* (online). Accessed August 10, 2022, https://digitalrepository.trincoll.edu/cgi/viewcontent.cgi?article=1028&context=hartford_papers

[19] 1870 US Census

[20] Ginty, "Broderick," 1.

[21] 1880 US Census.

[22] Taryn Phelan (online). Accessed August 10, 2022, https://tarynphelan.com/g0/p61.htm

[23] Ibid.

[24] https://tarynphelan.com/exhibits/broderick,-clement-1900-us-census.jpg

[25] Ginty, "Broderick," 2.

[26] "History of Unionville," Unionville Museum (online). Accessed July 9, 2022, https://www.unionvillemuseum.org/history-of-unionville.html

[27] *Hartford Courant*, June 20, 1913, 5.

[28] https://today.uconn.edu/2016/08/henry-monteith-portrait-grand-old-man/

[29] Ginty, 2.

[30] *Hartford Courant*, June 20, 1913, 5.

[31] *Hartford Courant*, July 18, 1903, 5.

[32] Memoranda prepared by Broderick for Archbishop Spellman, dated October 19, 1939; Bishop Broderick Collection, Collection Number 022.004, Box 1, Folder 5. Archives of the Archdiocese of New York, St. Joseph's Seminary, Dunwoodie. Hereafter, Memoranda of 1939. Archdiocese of New York Archives.

[33] Ibid., 3.

[34] Ibid., 3.

[35] *Boston Globe*, October 28, 1903, 7.

[36] Lawrence McMahon was born in St. John, Brunswick, Canada on December 26, 1835; ordained March 24, 1860; consecrated Bishop of Hartford August 10, 1879; died August 21, 1893.

[37] The friendship may have soured somewhat after Broderick's exile, as O'Connell was a protégé and lifelong intimate of Cardinal Gibbons.

[38] Bonaventure Finnbarr Broderick, *The So-Called Altar of Calvinus* (New York, 1940), 2.

[39] Memoranda of 1939, 1. Archdiocese of New York Archives.

[40] Michael Tierney was born in Ballylooby, County Tipperary, Ireland on September 29, 1939; ordained May 26, 1866; consecrated Bishop of Hartford, February 22, 1894; died October 5, 1908.

[41] "Assignments of Priests," *Meridian Daily Journal*, July 17, 1897, 5.

[42] "Cathedral Lyceum Notes," *Hartford Courant*, September 24, 1897, 12.

[43] "Honors for Irish and American Students", *The Monitor*, Volume 41, Number 15, January 15, 1898, 330.

[44] *The Hartford Courant*, February 24, 1898, 7.

[45] Yoshinobu Hakitani, ed., *Theodore Dreiser's Uncollected Magazine Articles, 1897-1902* (University of Delaware Press, 2003), 292-294.

[46] Ibid., 296.

[47] Ibid., 298.

[48] *The American Journal of Theology*, July 1898, Vol. 2, No. 3, 686-688.

[49] *Boston Globe*, Boston, MA, October 28, 1903, 7.

[50] Bonaventure Finnbarr Broderick, *The Forum Stele* (New York, 1940).

[51] "Academy of Arcadia, *Italian Accademia Dell'arcadia*, Italian literary academy founded in Rome in 1690 to combat Marinism, the dominant Italian poetic style of the 17th century. The Arcadians sought a more natural, simple poetic style based on the classics and particularly on Greek and Roman pastoral poetry." As found at https://www.britannica.com/topic/Academy-of-Arcadia

[52] Brendan A. Finn, *Twenty-Four American Cardinals* (Boston: Bruce Humphries, Inc., 1947), 152. "It has been said that Cardinal Mundelein was the first American to be admitted to this Academy, but that distinction belongs to another illustrious member of our American Hierarchy, Bishop Bonaventure F. Broderick, a native of Hartford, distinguished among other things, for his studies in Roman archaeology." Also see *Poughkeepsie Journal*, May 17, 1964. 10.

[53] "On 2 February 1879 the *Collegium Cultorum Martyrum* was established by M. Armellini, A. Hytreck, O. Marucchi ed E. Stevenson, leading experts on the Sacred aspects of the ancient world. Then through the ex-

press desire of Blessed John Paul II it was raised to the status of Pontifical Academy and connected to the Pontifical Council for Culture." (online). Accessed July 9, 2022. http://www.cultura.va/content/cultura/en/collegamenti/accademie-pontificie/cultorum-martyrum.html

[54] "The Bishop Bonaventure F. Broderick Collection of Ancient Coins," booklet catalogued by Frederick S. Knobloch, Manhattan College, New York City, 1942. Booklet in the possession of the author.

[55] *Boston Globe*, Boston, MA, October 28, 1903, 7. The seminary was located at 352 Collins Street in Hartford; the site was originally the Chinese College, then the Bowen School for Boys. The diocese abandoned the site in when a new, larger seminary was built in Bloomfield in 1928-29.

[56] Memoranda of 1939, 1. Archdiocese of New York Archives.

[57] "One Hundred Years," anniversary booklet of the parish, October 2, 1955.

[58] *Hartford Courant*, February 13, 1900, 8.

[59] Memoranda of 1939, 1. Archdiocese of New York Archives.

[60] Ibid.

[61] *Transcript-Telegram*, Holyoke, MA, July 18, 1903, 4.

[62] *Hartford Courant*, October 5, 1898, 3.

[63] "Stuck to his Contract," *North Adams Transcript*, February 27, 1899, 2.

[64] "Going to Windsor," *Hartford Courant*, May 8, 1898, 3.

[65] "Bishop Broderick on Witness Stand," *Hartford Courant*, June 20, 1913, 5.

[66] "Broderick Troubles," *Hartford Courant*, January 22, 1900, 5.

[67] Clement died four years later, in 1903, at age 37 on July 17, 1903.

[68] "Bishop Broderick on Witness Stand," *Hartford Courant*, June 20, 1913, 5.

[69] Ginty, "Broderick," 4.

[70] "Doctor Broderick's Plans," *Meridian Journal*, February 13, 1900, 9.

[71] Ibid.

[72] "Bishop Broderick on Witness Stand," *Hartford Courant*, June 20, 1913, 5.

[73] Finn, *Twenty-Four*, 346.

[74] "Pastor Sued," New Haven *Morning Journal Courier*, February 16, 1900, 2.

⁷⁵ *Waterbury Evening Democrat*, June 18, 1902, 1.

⁷⁶ David D. Jividen, "Vatican, Role in War," The Encyclopedia of the Spanish-American War (ABC-CLIO, 2001), 674.

⁷⁷ Ibid.

⁷⁸ The *Times of Philadelphia*, March 1, 1896, 18.

⁷⁹ Fort Wayne *Weekly Gazette*, March 5, 1896, 4.

⁸⁰ Ibid.

⁸¹ Ibid.

⁸² "The War of Desolation and Death in Cuba," Wilmington, North Carolina *Messenger*, May 15, 1897, 2.

⁸³ Frank T. Reuter, *Catholic Influence on American Colonial Policies 1898-1904* (Austin: University of Texas Press, 1967), 4-5.

⁸⁴ *Pastoral Letters of the United States Catholic Bishops, Volume I, 1792-1940*, Publication No. 880 (Office of Publishing Services, United States Catholic Conference, Washington, DC, 1984), 215-216.

⁸⁵ *The Weekly Bee*, Sacramento, California, May 25, 1898, 12.

⁸⁶ June 10, 1897, 4.

⁸⁷ Clay Risen, *The Crowded Hour: Theodore Roosevelt, the Rough Riders, and the Dawn of the American Century* (New York: Scribner, 2019), 187.

⁸⁸ Risen, *The Crowded*, 40.

⁸⁹ *Boston Pilot*, February 26, 1898, 4.

⁹⁰ Risen, *The Crowded*, 49.

⁹¹ Office of the Historian, United States Department of State, accessed July 9, 2022, https://history.state.gov/milestones/1866-1898/spanish-american-war

⁹² Reuter, *Colonial*, 13.

⁹³ Jose M. Hernandez, "Cuba in 1898," Library of Congress (online). Accessed April 15, 2022, https://www.loc.gov/rr/hispanic/1898/hernandez.html

⁹⁴ "Havana's Awful Condition," *The Kincaid Dispatch*, January 20, 1899, 1.

⁹⁵ *Boston Globe*, Boston, MA, October 28, 1903, 7.

⁹⁶ *Arkansas Democrat*, Little Rock, Arkansas, February 3, 1900, 3.

⁹⁷ Finn, *Twenty-Four*, 346.

⁹⁸ Ventura Fuentes, "Cuba." In *The Catholic Encyclopedia*, Vol. 4, 1908.

[99] Memoranda of 1939, 1. Archdiocese of New York Archives.
[100] Finn, *Twenty-Four*, 348-9.
[101] Memoranda of 1939, 1. Archdiocese of New York Archives.
[102] Ibid.
[103] *Times Democrat*, New Orleans, August 31, 1899, 3.
[104] Reuter, *Catholic Influence*, 45.
[105] Memoranda of 1939, 1. Archdiocese of New York Archives.
[106] Finn, *Twenty-Four*, 347.
[107] Ibid.
[108] Ibid., 53.
[109] *Boston Globe*, October 28, 1903, 7.
[110] "Papal Policy in Philippines," *Altoona Tribune*, December 14, 1901 2.
[111] Gerald Fogarty, *The Vatican and the American Hierarchy From 1870-1905* (Wilmington, Delaware: M. Glazier, 1985), 188.
[112] Broderick's Notebook, Bishop Bonaventure Broderick Collection, 022.004, box 1, folder 13. Archdiocese of New York Archives.
[113] "Bishop Broderick on Witness Stand," *Hartford Courant*, June 20, 1913, 5.
[114] Memoranda of 1939, 2. Archdiocese of New York Archives.
[115] "Havana's Triple Consecration," *Boston Globe*, Boston, MA, October 28, 1903, 7.
[116] *Naugatuck Daily News*, December 27, 1901, 2.
[117] William Henry Thorne, "Side Lights on Current Church History," *The Globe*, Volume XI, 1901, 473.
[118] Ibid.
[119] Reuter, *Catholic Influence*, 131.
[120] Letter from Broderick to O'Connell, February 10, 1902, MDRI 9 Broderick, University of Notre Dame Archives, South Bend, Indiana.
[121] Ginty, 16.
[122] https://portal.ct.gov/SOTS/Register-Manual/Section-VII/Population-1900-1960
[123] Ginty, 2.
[124] *Hartford Courant*, July 18, 1903, 5.
[125] *Hartford Daily Courant*, July 20, 1903, 7.
[126] *Naugatuck Daily News*, December 27, 1901, 2.

[127] "Havana's Triple Consecration," *Boston Globe*, Boston, MA, October 28, 1903, 7.

[128] A titular bishop is a bishop in title, not in charge of a diocese, including coadjutor bishops and auxiliary bishops. Being a bishop implies being head of a Christian Church; the title serves this purpose for bishops without full responsibility for a diocese and often memorializes ancient Churches which no longer exist in territories no longer Christian. In Broderick's case Juliopolis was an ancient city and episcopal see in Anatolia, modern-day Turkey. Provisions for the title are found in the Code of Canon Law.

[129] "Bishop Broderick on Witness Stand," *Hartford Daily Courant*, June 20, 1913, 5.

[130] Ginty, 15.

[131] Memoranda of 1939, 1. Archdiocese of New York Archives.

[132] Ibid., 2.

[133] Letter to Broderick from Elihu Root; Bishop Bonaventure Broderick Collection, 022.004, box 1, folder 7. Archdiocese of New York Archives.

[134] Letter from Archbishop J. G. Murray to Monsignor Keegan, January 11, 1939, Bishop Bonaventure Broderick Collection, 022.004, box 1, folder 5. Archdiocese of New York Archives.

[135] Ginty, 16.

[136] *Wall Street Journal*, January 19, 1899, 5.

[137] "Episcopology of the Catholic Church in Cuba" (online). Accessed October 13, 2022. https://cardinals.fiu.edu/obispos/bio-b.htm

[138] Memoranda of 1939, 2. Archdiocese of New York Archives.

[139] "Rev.Dr. Joseph P. Solignac is Busy With Archbishop's Private Papers," New Orleans *Times-Democrat*, August 15, 1905, 5.

[140] Scrapbook, Bishop Bonaventure Broderick Collection, 022.004, box 2, folder 1. Archdiocese of New York Archives.

[141] "Rev. Dr. Joseph P. Solignac is Busy with Archbishop's Private Papers," New Orleans Times-Democrat, August 15, 1905, 5.

[142] *Times-Democrat*, New Orleans, Louisiana, July 11, 1912, 1.

[143] Memoranda of 1939, 3. Archdiocese of New York Archives.

[144] Eau Claire, Wisconsin *Leader-Telegram*, April 25, 1905, 1.

[145] *The Catholic Telegraph*, Vol. 73, Number 51, 22 December 1904.

¹⁴⁶ *The Brooklyn Citizen*, December 18, 1904, 9.

¹⁴⁷ Ibid.

¹⁴⁸ Letter of Resignation, December 17, 1904, Bishop Bonaventure Broderick Collection, 022.004, box 1, folder 2. Archdiocese of New York Archives.

¹⁴⁹ Memoranda of 1939, 3. Archdiocese of New York Archives.

¹⁵⁰ "Peter's Pence: A History as Ancient as the Church," (online). Accessed October 13 2022: https://www.obolodisanpietro.va/en/cos-e-l-obolo/storia/storia-dell-obolo.html

¹⁵¹ List or Manifest of Alien Passengers for the U.S. Immigration Officer at Port of Arrival, List A, No. 5593.

¹⁵² Spellman asked for this explanation in 1939. Broderick provided a response under the heading "Why I did not remain in Rome at that time, December 1904, as suggested by the Holy Father, and by Archbishop Gasparri" in his Memoranda of October 17, 1939, 3. Bishop Bonaventure Broderick Collection, 022.004, box 1, folder 5. Archdiocese of New York Archives.

¹⁵³ Memoranda of 1939, 3. Archdiocese of New York Archives.

¹⁵⁴ "Monsignor Broderick to Establish New Bureau in Washington," *Catholic Union and Times*, Buffalo, NY, February 16, 1905, 1.

¹⁵⁵ Memoranda of 1939, 3. Archdiocese of New York Archives.

¹⁵⁶ *The Washington Post*, March 1, 1905, 21.

¹⁵⁷ Letter from Palma to Broderick, Scrapbook, Bishop Bonaventure Broderick Collection, 022.004, box 2, folder 1. Archdiocese of New York Archives.

¹⁵⁸ *The Philadelphia Inquirer*, March 5, 1905, 32.

¹⁵⁹ "Cardinal At Luncheon", *The Times-Picayune*, New Orleans, February 21, 1905, 5.

¹⁶⁰ *New York Times*, March 16, 1905.

¹⁶¹ "Treasurer Elected," *Washington Evening Star*, May 5, 1905, 12

¹⁶² John Tracy Ellis, *Catholic Bishops, A Memoir* (Wilmington, Delaware: Michael Glazier, Inc., 1983), 99.

¹⁶³ Doc. #102E in the Associated Archives at St. Mary's Seminary and University, Baltimore.

¹⁶⁴ Spellman's letter to Cicognani.

[165] Doc. #102F12, in the Associated Archives at St. Mary's Seminary and University, Baltimore.

[166] Archbishop Diomede Falconio.

[167] Bishop Bonaventure Broderick Collection, 022.004, box 1, folder 2. Archdiocese of New York Archives.

[168] https://babel.hathitrust.org/cgi/pt?id=nnc1.cu56779232&view=1up&seq=15

[169] https://libraryguides.missouri.edu/pricesandwages/1900-1909 accessed July 30, 2022.

[170] Memoranda of 1939, 3. Archdiocese of New York Archives.

[171] New York State Census, 1905. A.D. 25, E.D. 09, New York, New York, June 1. Listed as a "guest" and occupation "Clergyman."

[172] January 2, 1906, p. 8.

[173] https://www.worldhistory.org/article/1771/the-gilded-age-estates-of-staatsburg-new-york/ accessed April 12, 2022.

[174] Book 342, page 189, Dutchess County deed transfer records, 1905.

[175] *The Argus*, Albany, New York, October 31, 1905, 3.

[176] "Immigration to the United States, 1789-1930," (online). Accessed October 13, 2022, https://curiosity.lib.harvard.edu/immigration-to-the-united-states-1789-1930/catalog/39-990077727760203941

[177] "Wants Good Immigrants," *Baltimore Sun*, January 8, 1906, 10.

[178] The Washington Post, March 26, 1905, 2.

[179] Nan E. Woodruff, ed., *Booker T. Washington Papers Volume 9:1906-08* (University of Illinois Press, 1980), 508-510.

[180] Terence Vincent Powderly (1849-1924), the American labor leader, was mayor of Scranton, PA (1878-84), U.S. commissioner general of immigration (1897-1902), and chief of the division of information in the Bureau of Immigration (1907-21).

[181] According to historian and author Robert Barcio, Powderly "was a practicing Catholic until 1901 when he joined the Masons." *Cathedral in the Wilderness* (Diocese of Erie, 1991) 181.

[182] *The Washington Post*, November 10, 1905, 1.

[183] Risen, *The Crowded*, 26.

[184] *The Washington Post*, November 16, 1905, 12.

[185] *The Argus*, Albany, New York, October 31, 1905, 3.

[186] Atlanta *Constitution*, March 23, 1906, 14.

[187] *The Tampa Tribune,* February 7, 1906, 1.
[188] "Southern Peonage Stories," *The Sun,* New York, August 2, 1906, 4.
[189] Brad Ricca, "Mrs. Sherlock Holmes," (New York: St. Martins Press, 2016), 85-90.
[190] "Southern Peonage Stories," *The Sun,* New York, August 2, 1906, 4.
[191] Ricca, *Mrs. Sherlock,* 85-90.
[192] "Dutchess County," Poughkeepsie *Eagle,* November 6, 2006, 8.
[193] *The Sun,* October 28, 1906, 37.
[194] Book 352, page 205, Dutchess County deed transfer records, 1907.
[195] Margaret Broderick household, 1910 United States Federal Census, Westchester, New York, population schedule, Yonkers, ED 173, sheet 15A, dwelling 15, family 160.
[196] "Suit for $750,000 Grows out of Big Cuban Contracts," *Bridgeport Times and Evening Farmer,* Bridgeport, Connecticut, July 16, 1913, 2.
[197] *Who's Who in New York and State, Containing Authentic Biographies of New Yorkers who are Leaders and Representatives in Various Departments* (L.R. Hamersly & Co., January 1, 1907).
[198] An interesting sidebar: Father Thomas Ducey was an honorary pallbearer at Henry B. Plant's funeral. Ducey presided at the marriage of the under-aged son of presidential candidate James G. Blaine. Blaine threatened Father Ducey with legal action over the ceremony.
[199] "H. B. Plant's Widow a Bride," *New York Times,* January 20, 1904, 7.
[200] Kelly Reynolds, "Henry Plant, Pioneer Empire Builder," (Cocoa, Florida: The Florida Historical Press, 2010), 195.
[201] "Plant Millions Divided," *New York Times,* June 4, 1909, 15.
[202] "Bradish Johnson Estate Involved," *New York Tribune,* February 16, 1900, 11.
[203] "Villa Marguerite, Smart Principality," *Kingston Daily Freeman,* April 11, 1912, 2.
[204] "John Brezee has resigned his position as chauffeur for Bishop Broderick. Charles Maines succeeds him," *Kingston Daily Freeman,* February 4, 1911. "Charles Mains has severed his connection as chauffeur for Bishop Broderick," *Kingston Daily Freeman,* July 17, 1911. "Charles Sorge of Ulster Avenue has entered the employ of Bishop Broderick." *Kingston Daily Freeman,* August 7, 1911.

²⁰⁵ *Kingston Daily Freeman*, February 27, 1911.

²⁰⁶ *The Columbia Republican*, September 30, 1913, 8.

²⁰⁷ The well-known soprano Inez Barbour Hadley (Henry) was born in Pittsburgh in 1879, died in 1971, and is buried in Cambridge, MA

²⁰⁸ *Kingston Daily Freeman*, October 31, 1910.

²⁰⁹ Poultney Bigelow Paper 1855-1954, (online). New York Public Library Archives and Manuscripts. Accessed October 13, 2022, https://archives.nypl.org/mss/302

²¹⁰ Diary (not Broderick's), Bishop Bonaventure Broderick Collection, 022.004, box 1, folder 14. Archdiocese of New York Archives.

²¹¹ Ibid.

²¹² Ibid.

²¹³ Ibid.

²¹⁴ Ibid.

²¹⁵ Letter from Farley to Kenny dated February 14, 1912; Bishop Bonaventure Broderick Collection, 022.004, box 1, folder 2. Archdiocese of New York Archives.

²¹⁶ Diary (not Broderick's). Archdiocese of New York Archives.

²¹⁷ Ibid.

²¹⁸ Ancestry.com (online). Accessed July 13, 2022 https://www.ancestry.com/imageviewer/collections/61682/images/48917_302022005545_0027-00466?treeid=&personid=&rc=&usePUB=true&_phsrc=OiM90&_phstart=successSource&pId=195765

²¹⁹ Sisters of the Good Shepherd Archive, St. Louis, Missouri.

²²⁰ St. Louis *Globe-Democrat*, January 14, 1899, 12.

²²¹ Sisters of the Good Shepherd Archives, St. Louis.

²²² "Our Lady of the Charity of the Good Shepherd," Catholic Answers (online). Accessed July 27, 2022, https://www.catholic.com/encyclopedia/our-lady-of-charity-of-the-good-shepherd

²²³ Civil Report of Major J.R. Kean, Major and Surgeon, U.S.A., Superintendent, Department of Charities, Havana, Cuba, August 26, 1901.

²²⁴ "He Had Compassion on Them," (St. Louis, 1927), 119 -120.

²²⁵ Civil Report of Major J.R. Kean, Major and Surgeon, U.S.A., Superintendent, Department of Charities, Havana, Cuba, August 26, 1901.

[226] Broderick's Notebook, Bishop Bonaventure Broderick Collection, 022.004, box 1, folder 13. Archdiocese of New York Archives.

[227] "He Had Compassion on Them," (St. Louis, 1927), 120.

[228] *St. Louis Globe-Dispatch*, July 21, 1901, 21.

[229] Sisters of the Good Shepherd Archives, St. Louis.

[230] The article appeared in Pearson's Magazine, Volume 24, July 1910, 38-47.

[231] "Slander Charge Made by Priest," New Orleans *Times-Democrat*, July 1, 1912, 1.

[232] Pearson's Magazine, Volume 24, July 1910, 38-47.

[233] "Cuba's Richest Man Dead," *Washington Post*, December 30, 1911, 3.

[234] Telegram from Placide Louis Chapelle to Theodore Roosevelt. Theodore Roosevelt Papers. Library of Congress Manuscript Division (online). Accessed July 9, 2022. https://www.theodorerooseveltcenter.org/Research/Digital-Library/Record?libID=o40197. Theodore Roosevelt Digital Library. Dickinson State University.

[235] *Pearson's Magazine* (May 1913), 623.

[236] "Pearson's Magazine in Bankruptcy; Owes $100,000," *The Morning Call*, Allentown, PA, October 2, 1917, 10.

[237] Letter included in Affidavit of David Broderick, Supreme Court, 1913., p. 147-152.

[238] "Sulzer Courts Fullest Publicity," *Baltimore Sun*, August 24, 1913, 2.

[239] "Suit for $750,000 Grows out of Big Cuban Contracts," *Bridgeport Times and Evening Farmer*, Bridgeport, Connecticut, July 16, 1913, 2.

[240] "Tables Cleared for Broderick Case," *Hartford Courant*, Jun 11, 1913, 5.

[241] Ibid.

[242] 'Lawyers Wrangle in Broderick Case," *Hartford Courant*, June 12, 1913, 3.

[243] "Bishop Broderick on Witness Stand," *Hartford Courant*, June 20, 1913, 5.

[244] "Bishop Broderick and Cuban Contract," *Hartford Courant*, June 25, 1913, 5.

[245] "Brother Loses Suit to Bishop," *Boston Globe*, August 18, 1913, 2.

²⁴⁶ "Tables Cleared for Broderick Case," *Hartford Courant*, June 11, 1913, 5

²⁴⁷ The Garde was a Hartford hotel located at 370 Asylum Street.

²⁴⁸ "Tables Cleared for Broderick Case," *Hartford Courant*, June 11, 1913, 5

²⁴⁹ "Twenty and Ten Years Ago," *Kingston Daily Freeman*, August 17, 1933, 4.

²⁵⁰ "Announcements," *Hartford Courant*, October 4, 1914, 6.

²⁵¹ *Hartford Courant*, January 1, 1915, 5.

²⁵² "Make Bishop Defendant in $750,000 Suit," Poughkeepsie *Evening Enterprise*, July 17, 1913, 8.

²⁵³ "Cuban Contract Case out of Court," *Hartford Courant*, March 30, 1915, 4.

²⁵⁴ "Enjoins H.J. Reilly," *The Brooklyn Citizen*, September 18, 1913, 6.

²⁵⁵ "Sulzer a Tool, Says Broderick," *New York Times*, August 25, 1913, 1.

²⁵⁶ Ibid. 2.

²⁵⁷ William Shakespeare, "King Lear," act 3:2, 58-59.

²⁵⁸ "Blackmail and Forgery Intimated," *Lexington Herald Leader*, July 26, 1913, 7.

²⁵⁹ Impeachment of State Officials, OLR Research Report (online). Accessed October 13, 2022, https://www.cga.ct.gov/2004/rpt/2004-r-0184.htm

²⁶⁰ *Kingston Daily Freeman*, February 3, 1896, 2. Warren never occupied the property but in turn sold it within six months to Henry Schroeder of Brooklyn (see *Brooklyn Daily Eagle*, June 13, 1915, 48.)

²⁶¹ *Kingston Daily Freeman*, May 5, 1914, 10.

²⁶² *Kingston Daily Freeman*, February 3, 1916, 2.

²⁶³ "Give Beefsteak Fest at Woodland N.Y.", *Brooklyn Daily Eagle*, June 25, 1916, 49.

²⁶⁴ "City and County Red Cross Showing Results," *Kingston Daily Freeman*, May 7, 1997, 10.

²⁶⁵ "Committee Named for Saugerties," *Kingston Daily Freeman*, April 13, 1917, 3.

²⁶⁶ Ibid.

267 "Cantine's to Reopen," *Kingston Daily Freeman*, February 22, 1976, 57.

268 "Saugerties Holds Patriotic Meeting," *Kingston Daily Freeman*, April 11, 1917, 5.

269 *Burlington Free Press*, April 28, 1921, 2.

270 *New York Times*, July 17, 1918, 11.

271 Letter from Glynn to Broderick, Scrapbook, Bishop Bonaventure Broderick Collection, 022.004, box 2, folder 1. Archdiocese of New York Archives.

272 Broderick's Notebook, Bishop Bonaventure Broderick Collection, 022.004, box 1, folder 13. Archdiocese of New York Archives.

273 *Burlington Daily News*, August 30, 1917, 2.

274 "Balloon in North Hero," *Burlington Suburban List*, November 4, 1920, 5.

275 Brigitte Sion, "Protocols of the Elders of Zion," myjewishlearning.com (online). Accessed October 13, 2022, https://www.myjewishlearning.com/article/protocols-of-the-elders-of-zion/

276 *New York Times*, December 1, 1920.

277 *New York Times*, December 16, 1920, 16

278 The American Hebrew, Vol. 108, December 31, 1920, 220.

279 "Exposing the Protocols as a Fraud," *New York Times* (online). Accessed July 9, 2022, https://www.nytimes.com/2016/10/28/insider/1920-21-exposing-the-protocols-as-a-fraud

280 Ibid.

281 Essex Junction, Vermont *Suburban List*, October 21, 1948.

282 *Burlington Suburban*, June 19, 1924, 5.

283 *Brooklyn Daily Eagle*, April 18, 1926, 95.

284 Per letter mailed to that address by Pablo Desvernine, January 4, 1926, Bishop Bonaventure Broderick Collection, 022.004, box 1, folder 2. Archdiocese of New York Archives.

285 "Bishop Broderick Explains Status," *Poughkeepsie Eagle*, March 11, 1929, 10.

286 Ibid., 1.

287 Ibid., 10.

288 Arthur C. DeCelle, "25 Years Ago: Cardinal Spellman Befriended Catholic Clergyman in Millbrook," *Poughkeepsie Eagle*, May 17, 1964, 10.

[289] *New York Times*, May 25, 1933, 37.
[290] *New York Times*, December 23, 1938.
[291] *New York Times*, November 21, 1939, 43.
[292] "The Preservation and Reuse of Historic Gas Stations," National Park Service, U.S. Department of the Interior (online). Accessed October 13, 2022, https://www.nps.gov/tps/how-to-preserve/briefs/46-gas-stations.htm
[293] John H. Lienhard, "Engines of our Ingenuity," (online). Accessed October 13, 2022, https://www.uh.edu/engines/epi975.htm
[294] Unemployment figures from *The Forgotten Man*, Amity Schlaes (Harper Collins, 2007).
[295] As of this writing there remains an operating (Mobil) gas station located on the property at 2480 US Route 44, Salt Point, NY 12578.
[296] John Jeanneney and Mary Jeanneney, *Dutchess County: A Pictorial History* (Norfolk, Virginia: Donning Company, 1983), 143.
[297] Kevin DeMartine, conversation with author, July 22, 2022.
[298] Letter from Keegan to Murray, January 10, 1939; Bonaventure Broderick Collection, 022.004, box 1, folder 5. Archdiocese of New York Archives.
[299] *Millbrook Round Table,* October 7, 1938, 2.
[300] *Millbrook Round Table,* December 9, 1938, 2.
[301] Ibid.
[302] *Millbrook Round Table*, October 7, 1938, 20-21.
[303] "Letters to the Editor," *New York Times*, December 13, 1936, 113.
[304] Ginty, 21
[305] Ibid., 22.
[306] Ibid., 21.
[307] Ibid., 22.
[308] Ginty, 23.
[309] p. 3. The Nelson House was a hotel on Market Street in Poughkeepsie that historians record served as temporary White House offices whenever President Franklin D. Roosevelt came to visit Hyde Park. It was demolished in 2012.
[310] "Dr. Broderick Speaks," *Poughkeepsie News Eagle*, December 7, 1935, 2.

[311] Letter from Monsignor Robert F. Keegan to Archbishop John G. Murray dated January 10, 1939. Bishop Bonaventure Broderick Collection 022.004, box 1, folder 2, Archdiocese of New York Archives.

[312] Mark Donovan, "Gilded Age Hudson Valley Estates," (online). Accessed July 9, 2022, https://markhistorydonovan.blogspot.com/2021/04/the-homestead-worthingtons-played-key.html

[313] Ancestry.com (online). Accessed August 12, 2022.

[314] Ellis, *Catholic Bishops*, 142.

[315] Gannon, *Spellman*, 140.

[316] "Catholic Growth 239,287 Last Year," *New York Times*, April 28, 1939, 28.

[317] "An Uncommon Prelate," *New York Times*, May 14, 1966, 20.

[318] Each year on November 17 the daily Mass intention at St. Joseph Church, Millbrook, is offered for Bishop Bonaventure Broderick, requested by former pastor, Rev. Msgr. Gerardo J. Colacicco.

[319] The property became the Cardinal Hayes Home for Children operated by the Franciscan Missionaries of Mary.

[320] Gannon, *Spellman*, 146.

[321] Ibid., 146-149.

[322] Bishop Bonaventure Broderick Collection, 022.004, box 1, folder 5. Archdiocese of New York Archives.

[323] Gannon, *Spellman*, 146.

[324] Bishop Bonaventure Broderick Collection, 022.004, box 1, folder 5. Archdiocese of New York Archives.

[325] John Deedy, *Seven American Catholics* (Chicago: The Thomas More Press, 1978), 81.

[326] Jim Bishop, "Career of a Brilliant Churchman", Pittsburgh *Post-Gazette*, June 4, 1962, 27.

[327] John Cooney, *The American Pope, The Life and Times of Francis Cardinal Spellman* (New York: Times Books, 1984), 91.

[328] Fogarty, *Patterns*, 223.

[329] Letter from Murray to Keegan, Bishop Bonaventure Broderick Collection, 022.004, box 1, folder 5. Archdiocese of New York Archives.

[330] Ibid.

[331] Ibid.

[332] Letter from Murray to Spellman, Bishop Bonaventure Broderick Collection, 022.004, box 1, folder 5. Archdiocese of New York Archives.

[333] Letter from Keenan to Lynch, September 1939; Bishop Bonaventure Broderick Collection, 022.004, box 1, folder 5. Archdiocese of New York Archives.

[334] Letter from Cushman to Spellman; Bishop Bonaventure Broderick Collection, 022.004, box 1, folder 5. Archdiocese of New York Archives.

[335] Letter from McGuire to Spellman, Bishop Bonaventure Broderick Collection, 022.004, box 1, folder 5. Archdiocese of New York Archives.

[336] Letter from Broderick to Spellman, Bishop Bonaventure Broderick Collection, 022.004, box 1, folder 5. Archdiocese of New York Archives.

[337] As his name appeared in *The Official Catholic Directory*, P. J. Kennedy & Sons, New York.

[338] Gannon, *Spellman*, 150.

[339] "Well Known Engineer is Dead at 73", *Hartford Courant*, January 3, 1940, 4.

[340] Letter from Cicognani to Spellman; Bishop Bonaventure Broderick Collection, 022.004, box 1, folder 5. Archdiocese of New York Archives.

[341] Fogarty, *The Vatican*, 267.

[342] "Mabies Purchase Washington Farm," *Poughkeepsie Journal*, December 20, 1941, 4.

[343] Documents of the Senate of the State of New York, Volume 26, 1916. New York State Legislature.

[344] "Hospital Stone is Laid in Bronx," *New York Times*, June 21, 1937, 21.

[345] Ibid.

[346] Ginty, 31.

[347] Ibid., 32.

[348] Ibid.

[349] Ibid.

[350] *Lapis niger* (Latin: *black stone*). The *Lapis Niger* is an ancient shrine in the Roman Forum. Together with the associated Vulcanal (a sanctuary to Vulcan) it constitutes the only surviving remnants of the old Comitium, an early assembly area that preceded the Forum and is thought to derive from an archaic cult site of the 7th or 8th century BC. (Wikipedia)

[351] Bonaventure F. Broderick, *The So-Called Altar*, 2.

[352] Letter from Baskerville to Broderick, Scrapbook; Bishop Bonaventure Broderick Collection, 022.004, box 2, folder 1. Archdiocese of New York Archives.

[353] "Raoul E. Desvernine Dies at 74; Lawyer and Foe of New Deal," *New York Times*, June 3, 1966, 39.

[354] Cyril M. Dettling, O.P., "Theology for the Layman," *Dominican Journal* (online). Accessed July 2, 2022 https://www.dominicanajournal.org/wp-content/files/old-journal-archive/vol42/no3/dominicanav42n3theologythelayman.pdf

[355] "Raoul E. Desvernine Dies at 74; Lawyer and Foe of New Deal," *New York Times*, June 3, 1966, 39.

[356] Scrapbook, Bishop Bonaventure Broderick Collection, 022.004, box 2, folder 1. Archdiocese of New York Archives.

[357] Ibid.

[358] Gannon, *Spellman*, 151.

[359] "'Twas a Great Day," *Daily News*, March 18, 1941, 385.

[360] "Bishop O'Brien is Consecrated," *The Tablet*, May 25, 1940, 20.

[361] National Catholic Welfare Conference News Service, Press Release 40-3099, November 25, 1940, 19.

[362] "Degrees Conferred at Mount St. Vincent," *The Tablet*, June 7, 1941, 6.

[363] "Archbishop Spellman Offers Mass for Nun," Ibid., December 26, 1941, 4.

[364] *The Catholic Advance,* Wichita, KS, January 2, 1942, 4.

[365] "K. of C. to Observe 450th Landing of Columbus," *Kingston Daily Freeman*, October 1, 1942, 10.

[366] National Catholic Welfare Conference News Service, Press Release 41-1486, June 9, 1941, 36.

[367] *Catholic Advance*, September 26, 1941, 8.

[368] National Catholic Welfare Conference News Service, Press Release 42-2847, November 16, 1942, 27.

[369] *The Catholic News*, New York, NY, November 27, 1943, 2.

[370] "Spellman Opens New Hospital Unit," *New York Times*, March 16, 1942, 32.

[371] "Eight Carmelites Pronounce Vows," *The Tablet*, June 6, 1942, 15.

[372] *The Herald Statesman*, Yonkers, NY, June 15, 1942, 3.

373 "Mother Mary Rosarie Buried on Saturday," *The Tablet*, July 18, 1942, 2.

374 *The Tablet*, October 24, 1942, 19.

375 *The Catholic Advance*, Wichita, KS, "Two Departure Rites Held for 17 Maryknoll Missionaries," September 18, 1942.

376 Catholic News Service, Newsfeeds, 6 December 1943, 8.

377 Note from Broderick to Dougherty, Archdiocese of Philadelphia Archives, Philadelphia.

378 Sally Fitzgerald, ed., *The Habit of Being* (New York: Vintage Books, 1980), 163.

379 Appointed December 16, 1901.

380 Appointed September 16, 1901.

381 Broderick's Notebook, Bishop Bonaventure Broderick Collection, 022.004, box 1, folder 13. Archdiocese of New York Archives.

382 Hospital records.

383 Letter from Finn to Spellman, Bishop Bonaventure Broderick Collection, 022.004, box 1, folder 6. Archdiocese of New York Archives.

384 "Bishop Broderick Mourned at Rites," *New York Times*, November 21, 1943, 56.

www.ingramcontent.com/pod-product-compliance
Lightning Source LLC
Chambersburg PA
CBHW032113090426
42743CB00007B/333